Houses with Charm
SIMPLE SOUTHERN STYLE

Houses with Charm

SIMPLE SOUTHERN STYLE

Text and Photography by
SUSAN SULLY

RIZZOLI
NEW YORK

New York · Paris · London · Milan

Acknowledgments

BOOKS NEVER COME INTO BEING THROUGH THE DREAMS AND EFFORTS OF A SINGLE INDIVIDUAL, but rather, through the collaboration of many. In addition to thanking the homeowners who graciously shared their houses and gardens, I also thank the architecture, design, and landscape professionals who brought their highest skills to the featured residences. I extend my heartfelt gratitude to Charles Miers, publisher of Rizzoli International Publications Inc., editor Sandy Gilbert Freidus, and graphic designer Eric Mueller of Element Group for helping to transform my thoughts, words, and photographs into a book of beauty and charm. I also offer thanks to the photographers who allowed me to include their work in these pages.

PHOTOGRAPHY CREDITS: Erica George Dines, pages 10, 149–159, 170–181, back cover; Gordon Beall, reprinted with permission from Meredith Corporation, © 2010 Meredith Corporation, all rights reserved, pages 41–49; Jean Allsopp, pages 161–169; Erik Kvalsvik, pages 194–205.

First published in the United States of America in 2013 by Rizzoli International Publications, Inc.

300 Park Avenue South, New York, New York 10010

www.rizzoliusa.com

Text and photography © 2012 Susan Sully

2013 2014 2015 2016 / 10 9 8 7 6 5 4 3 2 1

Printed in China

ISBN 13: 978-0-8478-4007-6

Library of Congress Control Number: 2012954521

Project Editor: Sandra Gilbert | Graphic design by Eric Mueller/Element Group

CASEWRAP: *Hand-printed and hand-colored cotton in the Venetian tradition from Groves Bros.* PAGE 2: *Antique door panels combined with a fragment of pressed tin create a romantic headboard in a New Orleans bedroom. Although their patina appears antique, the painted metal pedestals used as bedside tables are new. Ruffled linen pillow shams, a grain-sack bolster, and a lightweight linen duvet dress the bed.* OPPOSITE: *A nineteenth-century English sideboard with primitive lines and a faux-marbre top adds low-key elegance to an island guest room.* PAGE 6: *Blue-and-white export china has long been a mainstay in Southern decorating, whether formal or relaxed. Here, freshly cut hydrangeas arranged in a twentieth-century Chinese jar bring the bounty of a surrounding garden inside.*

*Hunc librum Ericius Mueller
die natali quinquagesimo dedico.
Audeate scintillare.*

Contents

Spelling Charm

Many of the South's most celebrated houses are ornate in style and imposing in stature. The Georgian dwellings of Williamsburg, Federal houses of Charleston, and Greek Revival plantations of Natchez are considered the architectural jewels of the region. Prized monuments, they celebrate wealth and worldliness. Preserved in house museums and memorialized in books, the architecture and period decor of these buildings have done much to shape international impressions of a region with formal tastes and cultivated style.

But there is another side of Southern style that values comfort above stateliness, personal taste over any particular canon of style, and low-key, lighthearted decor above lavish finery. Best described by the word "charm," it can be found anywhere in the region—in historic cities and their outlying neighborhoods, along country roads, in the mountains, and on the coast. More an attitude than an aesthetic, Southern charm transcends time, finding expression in houses dating from the seventeenth century to the twenty-first century and in interiors that are both traditional and modern.

When I began looking for houses and gardens to feature in this book, I found it difficult to define the parameters of my search. Can the word "charming" be used to describe an Italian Renaissance–style garden? Could a house with Greek Revival moldings and ceiling medallions be called simple? Do houses filled with French antiques or Turkish kilims qualify as Southern? I discovered that the answer to all of these questions is yes, because simple Southern charm is not defined by appearances but by an unaffected spirit that puts people at ease.

In her New Orleans living room, lighting designer Julie Neill creates a study in texture and patina reminiscent of the chandeliers she fashions from wood, bronze, crystal, and gilt in her nearby studio. An antique inkwell with a pewter top, old books, and a painted iron lamp sit on top of a vintage table next to a Louis XV sofa with gilded wood and modern linen upholstery.

The word "charm" has many definitions, including the casting of a spell. Everybody knows what it's like to walk into a room and instantly feel enchanted. The troubles of the world seem to drop away and a sense of wonder and delight takes over. It's hard to know exactly what conjures this response—color, the quality of light, or the presence of objects assembled less for their value than for the memories they evoke. Trying to categorize the tangible factors that call forth this mood is pointless. There is only one thing to do—let your guard down and surrender to the spell.

A charming house is a disarming place. It immediately invites you to enter someone else's world—which is the ultimate kind of hospitality and one for which Southerners are renowned. A room with comfortable chairs, touchable objects, and beautiful artwork or views says, "Sit down and stay awhile." Gardens with paths of old brick that lead beneath rose-spangled arbors encourage abandon to aimless pleasure. A porch furnished with old wicker and cooled by summer breezes is a haven for indulgent pastimes like daydreaming, napping, or gazing into space.

ABOVE: *In an elegant cottage designed by Atlanta-based architect Norman Askins, a graceful window with Gothic tracery offers a glimpse of the master bedroom located at the rear of the house.* OPPOSITE: *Resembling an old-fashioned sleeping porch, this bedroom is a recent addition to a circa 1845 Alabama farmhouse owned by preservationists Barbara and Sonny Adkins. Originally an open porch, the room is now enclosed by walls of painted cypress and furnished with family pieces from the late Victorian period.*

The earliest known definition of the word "charm" suggests one way in which these places work their magic. Charm, related to the word "chirp," first referred to birdsong and its natural, spontaneous harmony. Birdsong usually hails each day with a single fluting call that soon multiplies into a full chorus. During drowsy afternoons, a hush falls and the birds seem to doze a bit. Then at twilight, the serenade begins again with music that is quieter and more contemplative than morning's song. Houses with charm have similar rhythms. There are rooms where a single object, such as a carved mantel or a four-poster bed, sings a bold melody. Layered with the plainer notes of unbleached linen curtains or primitive country antiques, their visual impact is balanced by simplicity. Some houses can be visually quiet, with unfussy furnishings and a serene palette that calms the senses. Even when a multitude of objects fills a room, the effect isn't necessarily cluttered or cacophonous. In such spaces, the varied parts come together in pleasing compositions.

Simplicity, like charm, also has many definitions. To be simple is to be innocent, modest, and without pretense, like a Southern vernacular cottage built by a country carpenter. It also means pure and unalloyed, in the manner of a house that clearly expresses its creator's personality or its region's vernacular style. "Uncomplicated" is another synonym that is easily applied to houses with architecture and furnishings that never shout, but only say, "Welcome home."

In *Houses with Charm*, a selection of sixteen residences reveals the varied ways Southern home-owners, interior decorators, architects, and garden designers employ the language of simplicity to create irresistible homes. Houses characterized by their use of honest materials, pared-down decor, unified palettes, and well-edited furniture and accessories are featured in a section called "Pure and Simple." Including a beach cottage on the South Carolina coast, an early twentieth-century overseer's cottage in rural Georgia, and a contemporary farmhouse-style retreat in Mississippi, they all lack ostentation and offer an abundance of appeal. Whether their rooms are furnished with flea-market finds or family heirlooms, mid-century modern furniture or primitive antiques, these dwellings all foster a relaxed and carefree way of life.

The residences included in "Simply Elegant" celebrate the more refined side of Southern charm. Although the chandeliers and French antiques in a New Orleans home are highly decorative, their formality

A nineteenth-century French provincial armoire with wire screens in the upper panels introduces feminine curves into the room's strong, handsome architecture. The owner and interior designer Regina Lynch applied a distressed glaze to a vintage French deer trophy with real horns and a wood head. Hanging above the mantel, the quirky piece adds whimsy to the room.

is balanced by glazed pine floors, white walls, and curtains of plain polished chintz. In a residence on the Maryland coast, Middle Eastern carpets introduce pattern, color, and exotic style to rooms whose board-and-batten walls are reminiscent of old-fashioned beach houses. And in a cottage-style residence in Atlanta with snug rooms, beadboard walls, and family antiques, tall niches with pointed arches and tracery windows add fanciful Gothic details.

Together, these houses show just how rich simplicity can be. Whether fancy or plain, colorful or monochromatic, traditional or contemporary, they are equally inviting. Although the charm of such houses, like magic, can never fully be explained, it is experienced on many levels as the senses are teased and the soul soothed. When you are in a charming place, you know it . . . and you never want to leave.

A large dormer window in this cozy attic guest bedroom overlooks the Blue Ridge mountains. Touches of European finery, including the window's Gothic-inspired cornice board and French toile, mix with a casual slipcovered armchair and plain country chest.

Pure AND SIMPLE

Many of the South's houses are elemental rather than elaborate in design. With straightforward architecture, honest materials, and uncomplicated decor, they say "live in me" rather than "look at me." Sanctuaries for life's simple pleasures, coastal cottages and mountain homes invite inhabitants to live in harmony with one another and their natural surroundings. Urban dwellings become serene retreats from the outside world when decorated as authentic—but well-edited—expressions of their residents' personalities. Although not fancy, pure and simple houses can include fanciful details—handmade quilts, quirky folk art, antler chandeliers, or even the unexpected finery of a gilt and crystal one. Rather than overpowering their settings, these add an element of charm to the quiet beauty of their surroundings. Whether modern or traditional, vernacular or urbane, minimalist or not, houses like these offer balm to both the senses and soul.

Pale blue walls, a graceful chandelier, and a pretty slip transformed into a piece of art add feminine charm to a New Orleans bedroom with a rugged exposed pine ceiling and a simple yet handsome mantel.

Mountain Folly

HIGHLANDS, NORTH CAROLINA

Southerners have long escaped summer's heat in rustic Blue Ridge Mountain homes that offer a cool and relaxed alternative to their more formal urban dwellings. Inspired by the vernacular architecture of the region's early settlers, these were often constructed from raw woodland materials including locust timbers, chestnut bark, and woven rhododendron branches. With heart-pine floors, wormy chestnut walls, and exposed timbers, mountain homes like these reflect their natural surroundings, right down to the antlers and taxidermied hunting trophies that frequently decorate their walls.

When Atlanta-based architect Norman Askins began searching for a mountain house in Highlands, North Carolina, he had a different look in mind. "I wanted an airy, old-fashioned cottage, not the typical twig-and-bear thing," he explains. His search soon led him to a modest gabled cottage designed in 1943 by well-known mid-century Atlanta architect Richard Aeck. Although the interior was clad in dark pine and the oak floor had aged to an unattractive shade of orange, the house's intimate proportions, simple details, and plentiful natural light provided the perfect ingredients for Norman to fulfill his vision.

The architect bought the house within twenty-four hours of seeing it and immediately set about refining its more rustic details. The transformation began with the application of a pale glaze to the oak floors and several coats of paint in shades of cream and gray to the walls. Norman also added a large screened living porch and moved the kitchen from the dark northern side of the house to a sunlit room overlooking the mountains. With walls of planks painted white with wide "nickel and dime" cracks between them, a rustic fireplace made from a single piece of stone, and a farmhouse sink, the new kitchen immediately acquired rural Southern charm.

Atlanta-based architect Norman Askins embellished the facade of this 1943 shingled cottage in Highlands, North Carolina, with a Gothic-inspired porte cochere with sides of garden lattice. Sited on a sloping lot, the simple cottage commands magnificent mountain views from its rear windows and back garden.

Within this setting, Norman and his wife, Joane, decorated, in a style that seems more northern European than Blue Ridge Mountain in appearance. "We chose the style because it made the house look so much fresher and brighter," says Joane, an interior decorator and antiques collector. At first glance, this Nordic strain might seem at odds with the region's more primitive aesthetic, but it recalls the picturesque Alpine styles invoked by early developers in Little Switzerland and other nearby resorts. "When they built the first inns and cottages, many local entrepreneurs looked to Switzerland and Bavaria for inspiration," Norman notes. "So traveling a little farther north to Scandanavia isn't too much of a stretch."

According to Joane, a native Texan, and Norman, an Atlantan, there's also something very Southern about the way they've

decorated. "There was rarely any grand design scheme for old-fashioned summer houses," says Norman. Instead, he explains, rooms were filled with a hodgepodge of furniture borrowed from more formal homes, mixed with wicker and homemade objects. Pieces of different ages and styles, some refined and some not, coexisted easily, creating a relaxed, unpretentious environment. Combining the occasional fine antique with

OPPOSITE: *Rough chestnut beams, most likely salvaged by the cottage's builders from a nearby barn, span the living room's ceiling. Cotton duck slipcovers add relaxed appeal to the room's elegant European antiques and Persian Sevas rug. Hanging from hand-forged iron rods, burlap curtains dressed up with tapestry trim exemplify the room's mix of rustic and refined details.* ABOVE: *Carved with stars and rosettes, upholstered in green mohair, and decorated with a pillow embroidered with vines and flowers, the nineteenth-century French daybed is an elegant reflection of the natural world framed by the large window beside it.*

ABOVE: *In the entrance hall, nineteenth-century English Coalport china hangs above a table Norman designed using a modillion from a demolished turn-of-the-nineteenth-century New York building. In the master bedroom beyond, green-and-white toile quilts form bed hangings that mirror the serene palette of the woodland setting.* OPPOSITE: *A carved Gothic Revival door and eighteenth-century English blanket chest introduce an Old World touch to the entrance hall, where plain moldings and plank walls reveal the cottage's modest origins. Blue-and-white export china long favored by Southerners complements the striped fabric covering the seats of nineteenth-century American chairs.*

simpler details, the Askins' house clearly expresses this casual eclecticism. In the living room, for instance, slipcovered chairs sit on a beautiful Persian rug, and a quaint nineteenth-century floor lamp shines down on an antique French daybed. A zinc table from a catalog store occupies one corner of the room, and an antique chest purchased from an online auction house stands against the opposite wall. United by a muted palette of grays, blues, and green that echoes the room's mountainous view, the disparate elements complement one another and their natural surroundings.

Many pieces in the house are cherished antiques, like the eighteenth-century English blanket chest in the front hall, which was one of the first pieces Joane acquired. The hall also includes a table Norman designed, using an architectural fragment from a turn-of-the-nineteenth-century building as its base. Many of the furnishings and decorative objects in the house resemble things that might have been passed down through a Southern family—Victorian china, antique fancy chairs, and a portrait which, though Russian, resembles a primitive American painting.

ABOVE: *The varying shades of pink found in the dining room's Victorian English tureens, wall-mounted china, and Russian folk portrait add rosy contrast to the overall blue-gray palette. Throughout the house, the Askinses painted walls and glazed floors in tones of gray and cream, creating a muted setting that does not compete with the surrounding natural world.* OPPOSITE: *Victorian English china, an Italian majolica centerpiece, and American fancy chairs resemble objects that a Southern family might have transported from town to dress up their mountain dining room. Such family heirlooms typically have been mixed with more relaxed art and furnishings like the room's naive nineteenth-century portrait and circular table spread with a matelassé quilt.*

As in many summer houses, there is also a lighthearted spirit to the design. Among the most fanciful things in the house is a large model of a Swedish church crowned with a tiny onion dome. Unexpected details also abound in the gardens that Norman has tended and embellished over the years. On the eastern side of the house, a sunny croquet lawn terminates in classically inspired exedra—a verdant semicircle of hydrangeas with a replica of a Roman bust in the center. In the terraced garden behind the house, obelisks and geometric boxwood hedges introduce a surprising element of eighteenth-century European formality to overflowing beds of roses, verbena, sedum, and daisies.

"I like to experiment with the cottage style when I'm here," says Norman, who designs both romantic country homes and classical houses for his clients. "I constantly play with ideas, finding out what feels right." With a mix of high and low, old and new, American and transatlantic styles, the result is a fanciful hideaway where nothing is too serious. "This," says Norman, "is a folly of a house."

ABOVE: *Although the copper pots are French and a collection of pewter vessels mixes English, American, and European pieces, the homemade plate racks that hold them, fashioned by Norman's brother Ross, resemble those of Southern country kitchens.* OPPOSITE: *Walls of wide painted planks, a fire surround cleft from a single block of local stone, and plain country antiques impart rustic charm to the kitchen Askins created by remodeling the ground-floor bedroom. Norman added a butler's pantry and powder room behind the kitchen, including a reclaimed circular window—a favorite motif of the architect.*

ABOVE: *Norman describes the style of the rear garden as "country baroque." Over the years, he has embellished it, anchoring the design with large boxwoods and adding low hedges pruned into scrolls and ovals. In contrast to the garden's informal plantings of sedum, daisies, roses, irises, and other Southern favorites, steel obelisks add a more formal element.* OPPOSITE: *Inspired by axial Roman gardens, Norman designed a semicircular exedra in line with the cottage's porch and croquet lawn. Unlike precise Roman plantings, however, this bower overflows with hydrangeas, rhododendron, and hostas that thrive beneath the shade of native trees.*

Ecru, Ecru

NEW ORLEANS, LOUISIANA

When Louisiana interior designer Regina Lynch first saw the uptown New Orleans cottage she now shares with her daughter, Destiny Cowdin-Lynch, it was painted sunflower yellow. Equally vivid hues prevailed inside the house. But ironically, the color that Regina and Destiny love most is not really a color at all. Co-owners of an antiques shop on Magazine Street called Écru, they prefer white, beige, and anything in between.

"In the early days of my decorating, everything was about jewel tones, leopard prints, and lots and lots of accessories," says Regina, recapping the unrestrained tastes of the 1990s. "Now I like things to be simple, with neutral colors that you don't tire of quickly." Even as a teen, Destiny shared this aesthetic, opting for painted French furniture and linen bedding over pink gingham and plaid. Not surprisingly, the mother-and-daughter team's home is filled with pale French and Swedish antiques, linen slipcovered furniture, and walls that veer only occasionally from white to whispery blue-green tones. In a city where mahogany, velvet, and gilt have enjoyed a long and popular reign, its light, bright rooms offer a welcome change.

Long before the Shreveport-based interior designer bought her second home in New Orleans, Regina began collecting antique furniture to use in clients' homes. Many of these pieces now furnish her New Orleans cottage, including a French provincial armoire that fits perfectly into a corner of the living room. Similar in tone to the glazed pine beams of the ceiling, the ivory-and-grisaille piece is more refined in texture and form than the room's rough timbers. Harking to New Orleans' European roots, it recalls the way Creole settlers infused Old World elegance into their more primitive colonial homes.

Built in 1870, the Lynches' uptown New Orleans home is a Creole cottage-style house with two front doors opening to a four-square arrangement of rooms. After she bought it, owner and interior decorator Regina Lynch painted the bright yellow facade creamy white and stripped green paint off the original pine shutters to add subtle contrast.

In a typical Creole cottage floor plan, the Lynches' two front doors open to an adjoining pair of rooms identical in shape and size. With high ceilings, plain yet handsome moldings, and large windows, the modestly sized rooms seem larger than they are. Painting walls off-white and leaving windows bare of curtains, Regina created a quiet space where the textures, shapes, and character of carefully chosen furniture and accessories seem to engage in conversation. On one wall, a darkly glazed painting of angel wings by Tony Mose hovers above a chest adorned with an antique crucifix. Above the mantel, a quirky French deer trophy with real antlers and a painted wood head looks down its nose in a friendly manner at a white cowhide rug.

"A neutral palette doesn't meant that a room will look monotonous," says Regina. "On the contrary, it draws attention to all the different elements that make it interesting." In the master bedroom, even though most of the architectural details and furniture are white, the decor is infused with nuance and surprise. A headboard of painted antique doors towers above a bed with nineteenth-century European linen pillow shams and a bolster sewn from an antique grain sack. An Italian bench with a dark leather seat and gilded baroque legs contrasts with a pair of pedestals adorned with garlands

Khaki-colored moldings complement the glazed pine ceiling of the living room. A simple slipcovered sofa and ottoman recede into the neutral setting, allowing the more decorative pieces to stand out. By removing its glass panes, Regina transformed an outdoor light fixture into a charming chandelier.

and bellflowers. Above it all, a chandelier of gessoed wood, gilt, antiqued iron, and pearly beads marry matte with gleaming finishes.

"When designing a room, I often find the perfect piece among the antiques I've already collected," says Regina. When she began decorating the long, narrow dining room that once served as a porch, she chose as its centerpiece an eleven-foot-long antique harvest table she'd purchased in France. Ideally shaped for the room, its painted pine surface complemented the reclaimed poplar shelves and exposed beams. Vintage French chairs with rush bottoms soon found their place around the table, and an antler chandelier, also from France, added the final rustic touch.

The dining room opens to a kitchen that also was once part of the porch. Natural light shines into the room from a skylight, bringing out the rich glow of reclaimed wood cabinets and French terra-cotta-tiled counters. Originally, the cottage ended at the kitchen, but now a connecting hallway joins it to a contemporary addition, where a great room with age-darkened cypress ceiling beams resembles the cavernous interior of an old carriage house. When the Lynches moved in, the room's walls were painted to match the floor of eighteenth-century terra-cotta tiles. Now, white walls reflect the light that pours in through French doors, drawing attention to the natural variations of the wood ceiling and hand-glazed tiles.

ABOVE: *Ecru represents the work of an anonymous artist from Mississippi who creates ethereal "slip paintings" like the one hanging above the master bedroom's mantel. With walls painted a shade that shifts throughout the day from pale blue to green to gray, the bedroom is one of only two rooms in the house that deviate from the Lynches' preferred neutral palette.* OPPOSITE: *A Julie Neill Designs chandelier of wood and iron with touches of gilt hangs from the master bedroom's exposed pine ceiling. With robust legs and tooled leather seat, a masculine antique Italian bench balances the feminine bedding and French crystal sconces.*

OPPOSITE: *Converted from a porch, the dining room's proportions dictated a long, narrow table like this nineteenth-century French harvest table. Vintage French chairs with rush bottoms complement the rustic surface of its painted plank top. Regina describes the graceful French antler chandelier as "the biggest surprise in the house." Beneath it, an antique French demijohn catches Vermeer-like light.* ABOVE: *Realistic porcelain vegetables fill an antique hand-hewn biscuit bowl placed on the antique harvest table. The combination of textures, shades of white, and natural materials like rush and wood are typical of the Lynches' trademark aesthetic.*

Defining a cozy seating area in the spacious room, Destiny arranged an oversized sofa in front of the fireplace. To create an intimate area for dining, she placed a long antique farm table from Hungary against its back. Regina surrounded the table with French rush-bottom chairs with tall ladder backs that work well within the high-ceilinged space. A talented decorative painter, she covered the chairs that were once colored glossy yellow with chalky milk paint. Next, Regina planned to paint over the rusty surface of the corrugated metal fence visible through the room's French doors—but her daughter said no. "She thought it looked trashy," says Destiny, "but I love the weathered patina and patches of old paint."

Building an arbor with jasmine-covered wire and white minilights, Destiny created what she calls her "little garden sanctuary" in the shade of the tin wall. Convinced at last of the backyard's funky charm, Regina couldn't resist adding a romantic touch. Taking a pair of French iron sconces intended for the store, she attached them to the corrugated metal, where they dress up the old-fashioned picnic table covered with pots of herbs. "Every space, however simple, needs something to catch your eye and capture your imagination," she observes.

A large oil painting by New Orleans artist Tony Mose hangs above the eighteenth-century French mantel in the great room. Once painted terra cotta, the room now has white walls and pale furniture that contrast with the rich tones of the exposed wood ceiling and tile floor.

Architecture Without Attitude

MADISON COUNTY, MISSISSIPPI

When clients commissioned Louisiana-based architect Ken Tate to design a rural retreat, they asked him to capture the humble charm of Florida's cracker cottages. With metal roofs to deflect the sun, plentiful windows to catch the breeze, and porches for shade, these simple homesteads functioned in easy harmony within the sultry climate. Inviting an uncomplicated manner of living close to nature, this Southern vernacular style perfectly suited the clients' desire for a place to rest and relax in the Mississippi countryside.

Tate, who combines a deep appreciation of Southern styles with an intuitive approach to combining them, quickly found himself tapping a variety of other regional archetypes as well. "I thought the house should resemble a Mississippi farmhouse," he says, "both to complement the setting and to resolve a major challenge—building a 2,500-square-foot house without dominating the landscape." Emulating old farmhouses that gradually acquired additions and outbuildings, Tate designed a house that seems to ramble a bit, conforming to the undulating landscape instead of standing brashly on top if it.

Divided into three parts joined by sheltered passageways, the house appears from a distance to be a cluster of separate buildings. Varied in shape and size, each piece is crowned with a distinctly different type of roof, from the carport's low pyramid and the bedroom wing's hipped roof to the broad, broken-pitch roof of the main structure. While the smallest of these three components resembles an agricultural outbuilding, the largest assumes the iconic appearance of a Deep South farmhouse, right down to the porch that wraps

Beneath the living and dining room area's sixteen-foot ceilings, the modest proportions of country antiques introduce a cozy scale. Oak floors, sisal rugs, and wood furnishings, both painted and plain, add warmth to the expansive, brightly illuminated room.

OPPOSITE: *On either side of the parged brick chimney, doors fitted with screens open to a wraparound porch commanding 360-degree views. Between the porch's square posts, louvered blinds inspired by Creole architecture help to deflect the midday sun.* ABOVE: *Architect Ken Tate designed this family retreat in rural Mississippi to resemble a farmhouse with multiple additions. Both the residence and pool house are crowned with old-fashioned galvanized tin roofs that reflect the sun and keep interiors cool. Although traditional vernacular styles inspired the compound, the rhythmic geometry of its elements express a subtly modern aesthetic.*

around all four sides. Unlike an old country home, however, the primary structure consists of only one large living space, with the bedrooms separated in a discrete wing.

With a galvanized tin roof, square porch posts, and white clapboard walls, the architectural language of the exterior is traditional, but the concept behind the main mass's interior is far more modern. "I envisioned a grand but primitive salon that was all about the scale, the light, and the views," says Tate. With sixteen-foot-high ceilings and an open floor plan, the twenty-two-by-thirty-three-foot room is much larger than those found in typical rural dwellings. Heavy exposed studs underscore the rustic aspect of the "salon's" design, but the geometric grid they form on top of bare diagonal sheathing suggests a dynamic and contemporary aesthetic.

Ten pairs of French doors open from this room to the wraparound porch and landscape beyond. Inspired by the Mississippi and Louisiana Creole plantations that have long captivated Tate, the doors reveal a third influence at play. Like those of Creole plantations, the doors provide multiple ways to enter and exit the room, breaking down the boundaries between the interior space and porch that

ABOVE: *White-on-white studs and sheathing give the walls of the house an almost sculptural quality.* OPPOSITE: *The galley kitchen resembles one that might have been added to an old farmhouse when modern plumbing, electricity, and appliances became available by enclosing a corner of the porch. Double-hung windows, simple cabinets, Formica counters, and a painted wood floor resembling linoleum tile all support this fictional history.*

surrounds it. Fitted with screens, they are often left open to capture the breeze, and even when closed, their glass panes frame expansive views in four directions.

The residents furnished the large space sparely but comfortably, creating a dining area with a plank-top table surrounded by hand-painted spindle-back chairs. Warm in tone, old-fashioned in style, and relatively small in size, the chairs introduce a human scale within the expansive surroundings and create an intimate "room within a room." In the adjoining sitting area, a pair of deep sofas slipcovered in white that face each other across a plain pine table define another area that embraces those within it without enclosing them.

There is no art hanging on the room's walls or television concealed within a cabinet. "Nature is the only art," says Tate, who decided to leave the mantel off a fireplace surrounded by a floor-to-ceiling expanse of stuccoed brick. Ornamented only by variations within the parged brick, the eleven-foot-wide chimney wall seems almost to disappear between the glass doors that frame it. "A mantel would have drawn attention to the architecture," he explains. "I wanted the room to feel like a pavilion set within the landscape."

Traditional building materials and methods including exposed studs and diagonal sheathing, a painted board ceiling, and a parged brick chimney wall create an uncomplicated and relaxing environment in the living room. Pierced with ten pairs of tall French doors topped by transoms, the unadorned walls accentuate the surrounding views.

In the adjacent bedroom wing, exposed studs and sheathing echo the primitive-modern aesthetic of the living and dining room area. Country antique dressers and tables add the warmth of old pine to the white rooms, where pastel and white linens dress up iron bedsteads. In the small bedroom shared by three sisters, a trio of plain Victorian beds recalls the simple dormitories of old-fashioned summer camps. "I never told my clients, but at times I intentionally recalled the unaffected appearance of the South's early twentieth-century camps and summer compounds," says Tate.

This inspiration is most evident in the covered pool building beside the lake. With a broad pyramidal roof that dwarfs the plain posts of its screen walls, the building is intentionally primitive. "This is architecture without attitude," says Tate, describing the common denominator uniting the varied vernacular styles evoked throughout the property. Like the cracker cottages, country farmhouses, and plain camp structures that inspired its design, this family retreat is an unpretentious place where people come together to enjoy the natural beauty of the countryside in companionship with one another.

ABOVE: *Victorian iron beds and a few country antiques are the only furnishings in a bedroom shared by three sisters. The room's intentionally spare decoration evokes the simplicity of old-fashioned summer camps.* OPPOSITE: *Vintage wooden building blocks and wildflowers arranged on a country antique table add touches of color to an otherwise white bedroom in the rustic lakeside house.*

Coastal Magic

ISLE OF HOPE, GEORGIA

Isle of Hope is an enchanted place that seems to have slipped into a fold in time. Just a few fortunate souls live on the tiny island outside Savannah, Georgia, enjoying a slow pace of life in harmony with nature. Charming cottages line its quiet streets and on Bluff Drive, a winding road that hugs a bend in the Intracoastal Waterway, graceful antebellum homes overlook a wide expanse of sparkling water. In a town with no streetlights, only moonlight dappled by a canopy of old oak trees illuminates the night.

In the days before modern transportation and medicine, Isle of Hope was an easily accessible destination for citizens of Savannah escaping summer's heat and yellow fever epidemics. During the nineteenth century, wealthy planters, cotton factors, and merchants built homes on the land once belonging to nearby Wormsloe Plantation. Many of these were grand, designed in the popular Greek Revival and Italianate tastes, but other, less showy dwellings revealed the influence of Southern vernacular styles. One such house—an 1860 Lowcountry cottage with a raised brick foundation and red tin roof—captured the imagination of Atlanta residents Lisa and Vincent West when they explored the island several years ago. Like most homes on Bluff Drive, from which residents rarely move, the house was not for sale. But a week later, it unexpectedly became available and the Wests made their bid.

"I loved the simple style of the cottage and the airy atmosphere of its high ceilings and two-story porch," says Lisa. "It's very much of a traditional Lowcountry house." Vincent, whose family is in the lumber business, was just as enamored by the house's longleaf-pine floorboards and ceiling joists, which date from the mid-nineteenth century. "We wanted to keep as much as possible of the original house intact," says Lisa, who, with Vincent, commissioned Savannah-based architect John Deering to restore it, renovate the carriage house,

In a sheltered corner of the front porch, a hanging teak daybed with plentiful pillows becomes an inviting swing. Interior decorators Carter Kay and Nancy Hooff chose obsidian-colored paint for the floors and shutters, which, combined with melon-colored upholstery, injects modern style into the old-fashioned setting.

design a new guest cottage. They also engaged Carter Kay and Nancy Hooff of Carter Kay Interiors, who decorated the rooms and designed surfaces inspired by vernacular tradition to replace the gypsum board walls added by previous residents.

"The house told us what it wanted us to do," says Nancy, who suggested removing the dining room's dropped ceiling to reveal rugged floor joists above. The designers also commissioned decorative painter Bob Christian to cover its walls with a sepia-toned mural of live oak trees and salt marshes. "Lisa didn't want anything fancy in the room," says Carter. "Nothing more than a dining table and chairs." In keeping with their client's pared-down vision, the designers commissioned a twelve-foot-long table that nearly fills the space. Made from worn but polished reclaimed chestnut boards, the table comple-

ments the unpainted wood of the ceiling and mantel. Surrounding it with casual wicker seats, the designers chose modern end chairs with linen slipcovers to add a touch of elegance.

French doors with panes of antiqued mirrored glass open from the dining room to a kitchen that preserves its nineteenth-century predecessor's rustic atmosphere. Large windows bring light and breezes into the space, and a brick fireplace with a pine mantel darkened by years of smoke heats it in fall and winter.

OPPOSITE: *The ground-floor porch provides a cool, private place to enjoy outdoor meals or simply sit and swing. Before Carter and Nancy added a hanging daybed, the area beneath the front steps was an awkward, empty space.* ABOVE: *Shaded by the graceful limbs of live oak trees, this Southern vernacular–style cottage was built outside Savannah, Georgia, in 1860 as a summer house. "I'd always wanted a historic home," says owner Vincent West, "but I didn't want to be trapped in an urban setting. Isle of Hope is one of the few places where you can have a historic house, enjoy a sense of community, and still be on the water."*

OPPOSITE: *At Carter and Nancy's suggestion, the dining room's dropped ceiling was removed, exposing original longleaf-pine joists and trusses. Lending a casual appearance to the room, the change draws attention to the solidity and integrity of the house's original construction.* ABOVE: *A replica of a simple Greek Revival mantel found elsewhere in the house replaces a reproduction French-style mantel. Primitive creamware jugs and convex mirrors are among the few decorative accessories in the room where a scenic mural painted by Bob Christian provides the art.*

Beneath the ceiling's rugged beams and joists, a large island fashioned from antique heart pine creates a gathering place where the family often cooks together and shares informal meals.

When the Wests bought the house, the upstairs parlor had Sheetrock walls covered with red paint and trimmed with a decorative border. Now, pine boards cut to random widths with visible cracks between call to mind the stacked plank walls of vintage Lowcountry cottages. Painted a creamy shade of white, they reflect the light that flows in from the wide front porch through two pairs of French doors. The large space serves both as a sitting room for Lisa and Vincent, whose bedroom is next door, as well a popular gathering place for family and friends.

Most evenings, however, everyone ends up on the front porch, watching sunset reflections on the water and greeting neighbors who pass by. Vincent claims to have met more neighbors in two years on Isle of Hope than after three decades in Atlanta. In the late afternoon, he and Lisa enjoy watching the porpoises that swim past the screened pavilion at the end of their dock. But the couple's favorite time and place is their after-dinner stroll beneath the Spanish moss–strewn oaks of Bluff Drive. "When you are on Isle of Hope," says Vincent, "the weight of the world drops away."

Inspiration for the kitchen's design came from the texture and tones of its original building materials. Painted shelving matches the grout of the handmade brick chimney and an island of antique heart pine echoes the grain of the old mantelpiece.

ABOVE: *With a pair of antique tête-à-tête sofas, an eighteenth-century mirror, and a chandelier with cascading strands of ball chain, the parlor assumes a sexy, sophisticated air at night.* OPPOSITE: *Crowning painted pine planks with a coved molding, architect John Deering created the perfect backdrop for the living room's casual but stylish decor. New pieces with traditional lines complement antiques that include a nineteenth-century huntboard that Vincent inherited. With a modern Empire-style chandelier, grass blinds, a sisal rug, and sophisticated palette of ivory and terra cotta, the room is both elegant and down-to-earth.*

ABOVE: *In a small bedroom, the designers created an airy look with contemporary metal beds that recall the tall canopy frames of traditional plantation-style beds. The sheen of quilted polished cotton pillow shams and comforters contrasts with the room's natural linen coverlets and seagrass rug.* OPPOSITE: *Sunlight reflects off the red tin roof of the boathouse beyond the bedroom window, casting a rosy afternoon light. The room's restful, monochromatic palette is carried out in a variety of textures and finishes, from the burlap-covered headboard to the shiny painted floor.*

Reclaiming the Past

RICHMOND HILL, GEORGIA

The cottage that automobile magnate Henry Ford built in the late 1920s for the overseer of his Georgia lettuce farm is a simple house designed for a simple lifestyle. So says its current owner, Atlanta lawyer Harry Morgan, who slips off to this humble getaway with his wife, Vanita, whenever possible. The couple discovered the house in 1999 when they began searching coastal Georgia for a place to build a second home and family vacation cottage. Their explorations led them to the Ford Plantation, a low-density residential and sporting community twenty minutes south of Savannah.

Henry Ford purchased 80,000 acres of rice fields and timberland in the area in the 1920s, transforming the property into a winter retreat and flourishing produce farm. In 1998, a portion of it became the Ford Plantation, where the entrepreneur's Greek Revival–style mansion now serves as the community's gathering place. Surrounded by historic live oak trees and piney woods on the banks of the Ogeechee River, the house is one of the few original buildings to survive. The farm overseer's cottage is another of these, but when the Morgans discovered it, the dilapidated structure was slated for demolition.

"There was something about the run-down building that tugged at our hearts," says Vanita, "especially when we learned of its connection to the area." With a little encouragement from his wife, Harry began to appreciate the cottage's assets, particularly its history as a relic from Ford's time as well as its tiled roof, a rarity for the region. "If the roof had been made of tin or shingles, it wouldn't have had the same appeal," says Harry, who learned that the clay tiles were manufactured in nearby Ludowici, Georgia, in the 1920s. "I appreciated that Ford found the tiles near here, liked them, and used them—and that they have survived all these years," he says.

A bamboo hallstand positioned just inside the front door provides a place for the family to stash outdoor gear without cluttering the cottage's rooms. Although the Ford Plantation is a coastal marshland refuge for migrating birds and native wildlife, vintage decoys in the cottage's living room recall the Lowcountry's hunting traditions.

63

Originally, the cottage measured twenty-four feet square, with four compact rooms to which a kitchen and bathroom had been added. With the Morgans' addition of another bathroom and a porch overlooking the lake, it's still not much larger today. All the same, Harry and Vanita both hesitate to use the word "small" when describing the house. "I prefer 'intimate' or 'personal'—something that connotes a feeling of warmth," says Harry. "It never feels crowded, even when all the grandchildren are here."

When the Morgans began their restoration, most of the interior's original tongue-and-groove paneling was intact, covered with many coats of paint. Asking the workmen to leave vestiges of the paint for character, Vanita had the walls and ceilings sanded. The living room's Federal-style mantel was also stripped to expose the pine's grain and warm natural color. The most refined architectural element in the cottage, the mantel dresses up the brick fireplace that once heated the entire house with the aid of the kitchen's wood-burning stove. Furnished plainly with comfortable seating, a mix of vintage tables and lamps, and colorful folk art, the living room reflects the architecture's unpretentious style. "We had fun scouting roadside flea markets and antiques shops for pieces that might once have been in the house," says Vanita, who collaborated on the decoration with interior designer Suzanne Watson.

The 1927 cottage's board-and-batten siding and foursquare plan are typical of Southern vernacular style, but the original clay tile roof is unusual for the region.

ABOVE: *A light fixture assembled from vintage parts by lighting designer Eloise Pickard hangs above a 1950s table with a lazy Susan that is ideal for family meals. Although it appears old, the glass cupboard in the corner was constructed recently from recycled wood and a reclaimed window. French doors opening to a porch give the small dining room a feeling of spaciousness.* OPPOSITE: *When the Morgans restored the cottage, they raised the kitchen's ceiling and paneled it with pine salvaged from the lettuce barn that once stood across the street. Adding an enameled iron sink manufactured in 1950, they preserved the kitchen's vintage appearance. Vanita found an antique glass-fronted cabinet to fit in one corner of the room and designed a plate rack that complements the kitchen's period style.*

More of Vanita's finds decorate the dining room, including a tall pine hutch and homemade table with a lazy Susan. Here the couple often sets up a pair of laptop computers while grandchildren sprawl on the floor or perch in tiny chairs, playing with board games stored on the hutch's lowest shelf. Though not large, the room has an expansive feeling, thanks to French doors that open to a screened porch added by the Morgans. When planning the porch, Vanita envisioned it with a gabled roof, but after she consulted architect Jim Strickland of Historical Concepts, he made an alternate suggestion. Inspired by Southern vernacular tradition, he sketched a shed-roof porch better suited to the modest proportions and rural style of the house.

The Morgans also consulted Strickland on the design of a new guest bathroom addition. "We could easily have built something too big or tall," Harry says. The couple relied entirely upon their own understanding of the house's proportions and vernacular style when they renovated the cottage's original bathroom as the master bath. Although they increased the room's size, they kept the windows in their original locations, and when they installed new tongue-and-groove paneling, they matched the random-width boards found elsewhere in the house.

ABOVE: *Replacing the cottage's dilapidated bathroom with a new master bath, the Morgans added a raised ceiling of richly grained reclaimed heart pine. A reproduction claw-foot tub and a new vanity designed by Vanita are perfect period-style complements to the antique brass towel rack and dressing table.* OPPOSITE: *Vestiges of original paint add soft patina to the random-width tongue-and-groove walls of the master bedroom. Purchased at a shop in the nearby town of Richmond Hill, charmingly naive paintings of birds bring the outdoors inside.*

In the hallway outside the bathroom, heavy pine doors with original iron hardware open to the cottage's two bedrooms. Although both rooms are small, there is just enough space for bedroom essentials. Two antique side tables squeeze in on either side of a reproduction iron-and-brass bed in the master bedroom. In the guest room, vintage-style wall lamps mounted above a pair of brass twin beds eliminate the need for bedside tables entirely. With a sheer veneer of cool green paint on the walls, the room is a restful refuge for visiting family and friends.

Even when three generations are in the cozy house, there is still enough room for everyone. "There is something warm and comfortable about the cottage," says Vanita. "It invites a kind of family interaction that doesn't always happen in a larger house." These family get-togethers remind Harry of childhood summers spent at his aunt's house on nearby Tybee Island. Now, he enjoys sharing with his grandchildren the pursuits he loved as a boy—fishing, crabbing, and watching birds. When he and Vanita take long walks beneath the canopy of old oak trees, some planted in the 1700s, they are reminded of an even deeper past. "Being here gives us a true connection with a long-gone, less complicated way of life," says Vanita.

ABOVE: *Designed by architect Jim Strickland of Historical Concepts, the porch is a perfect place to enjoy the cooling breezes that waft over Lake Clara. Ceiling fans move the air when the breeze dies down, and when the brilliant coastal sunsets fade, an electrified kerosene lantern softly illuminates the table.* OPPOSITE: *Vanita designed a small golf cart garage and storage outbuilding in the style of the utilitarian dependencies that might once have stood on the lettuce farm. Inspired by the dovecotes popular in the rural South, the cupola adds an authentic detail.*

Garden of Delight

DECATUR, GEORGIA

"Simple" is not the first word that comes to mind when speaking about Ryan Gainey. Passionate, exuberant, romantic, whimsical—these are just a few adjectives that have been used to describe the internationally known gardener, designer, and Southern eccentric par excellence. But Ryan began life simply in a small South Carolina town, where he and his family shared a four-room house with a large vegetable patch and no indoor plumbing. Today, after a decades-long career, Ryan still lives in a modest Southern vernacular dwelling—a 1905 wood-frame cottage where the bathtub is located in an enclosed corner of the back porch and the shower is a short stroll away in an old greenhouse.

With heart-pine floors and walls of original plaster and tongue-and-groove paneling, the house remains close to the way Ryan found it in 1982. Reminiscent of the rural cottages he knew as a child, it's furnished with nineteenth-century oak and pine wardrobes, chests, and chairs, brass beds, and hand-sewn quilts. Into this setting, Ryan has mixed pieces of his own design—painted window cornices, an iron chandelier, and a table of reclaimed barn wood set with hand-painted earthenware. Even though made in recent years, these objects enhance the house's old-fashioned charm. "Almost everything I do has a rustic quality," says the designer.

The vine-covered cottage is located in the town of Decatur, Georgia, just outside the city of Atlanta, where Ryan operated several shops featuring plants, decorative objects for the home, and garden accessories. Author of *The Well-Placed Weed* and *The Well-Set Table*, the designer also created gardens for public and private clients and fashioned some of Atlanta's most important parties, including events for the Atlanta

Concrete coping stones from the original nursery's raised beds pave the pathway in the pair of adjoining gardens designed by Ryan Gainey. Strewn with petals from an arbor of 'New Dawn' roses, the tunnel-like passageway leads to a formal geometric garden. At the entrance to the circular garden, terra-cotta pots made by the Hewells, a seven-generation family of Georgia potters, are planted with standard iceberg roses.

Botanical Garden, the High Museum of Art, and the International Olympic Committee. But Ryan's greatest and most celebrated achievement may well be his own private garden, a two-acre piece of land that he has shaped and tended over a period of thirty years.

Ryan purchased the property where his cottage and garden lie in the 1980s from a family who supplied plants to his businesses. When he acquired it, the nursery included several raised beds and five greenhouses, two of which remain. Ryan dismantled the rest, transforming their sites into a series of garden rooms, each with a distinctly different character. Adding boxwood parterres and topiaries, rose-covered arbors, walls of old brick, and Tennessee stone pavings, he gradually transformed the country nursery into a cultivated—but never primly manicured—domain.

"I have tried to maintain as much as possible of the property's material and history," says Ryan, who paved a path in a space called the Borders with coping-stones from an original raised bed. More a passageway than a destination, the Borders is a sun-dappled tunnel beneath a fragrant arbor of roses and jasmine that terminates in a geometric boxwood garden.

An antique panel of stained and painted glass depicts a cluster of sunflowers—Ryan's chosen emblem. The walls of the room are densely covered with family pictures, certificates, diplomas, and photographs from events and theatrical productions in which Ryan has taken part. A broom he made as a child with a beloved aunt hangs beside the fireplace beneath her straw gardening hat.

Combining formal axial design with informal plantings of hydrangeas, crepe myrtles, and heirloom roses, these adjoining rooms perfectly express Ryan's dual passions for classical and cottage garden styles. "I'm deeply rooted in what I call the romantic garden style," he says, "but at the same time, I'm enamored of Italian Renaissance garden design."

On the far side of the property, a low wall of reclaimed brick encloses another garden room. In the wall's center, a gate opens to a gravel path where a terra-cotta urn flanked by putti forms a focal point. Lead ornaments shaped like pineapples stand on the wall, framing the gate Ryan fashioned from a piece of Haitian metalwork that depicts the Tree of Life. While the lead pineapples are larger than those found in nature, the classical temples arranged beside them are miniature replicas of antique buildings. Designed by Ryan, each has different capitals representing the four seasons of a garden, with fiddlehead ferns, sunflowers, ears of corn, and oak leaves with acorns.

A bower of roses and lonicera vines, plumes of euphorbia planted in an Italian wall urn, and two cotinus with leaves of purple and gold surround the gate. "I love to combine these colors," says Ryan. Associating gold with Apollo and purple with Dionysus, the garden philosopher sees the marriage of the two as a metaphor for the balance between passion and reason, voluptuousness and restraint—opposites that

ABOVE: *A portrait of the designer's mother stands on an antique pine chest.* OPPOSITE: *Antique botanical prints and hand-painted window cornices with a pattern of vines designed by Ryan bring the garden inside the ground-floor bedroom. A late nineteenth-century wardrobe contains a collection of bespoke clothing, including the dramatic robelike dusters of linen and silk that Ryan is known for wearing.*

define the human condition and his own garden aesthetic. "The psyche responds to color, even though most people aren't conscious of it," he says.

A rustic frame of locust timbers surrounding French-style topiary gives the garden room called the Arbors its name. Diamonds, spheres, and cones of boxwood form parterres that run the length of the narrow space. Zigzagging paths of pea gravel add more geometry, but garlands of gardenia roses and lush stands of woodland ferns tip the scale over to the romantic side. A shady bower of green and white by day, the room grows mysterious at night when hand-painted lanterns illuminate its mazelike paths.

"I'm deeply involved in the effect my garden design has on people," says Ryan, who plans to work on his garden for the duration of his life. "All my works are unfinished *tableaux vivants*," he says, likening his gardens to posed arrangements of costumed actors depicting histories and allegories. A living picture that shifts and changes throughout the seasons and years, Ryan's garden speaks both of the mercurial spirit of its creator and of the historical sources that inspire him. "I'm a garden evolutionary," says Ryan, "not a revolutionary."

Although they resemble primitive country antiques, the table and chairs in the dining room were designed by Ryan and constructed from reclaimed barn flooring. The table is set with hand-painted earthenware in a pattern by Ryan called "The Gathered Garden." Each plate depicts a different vegetable, including asparagus, aubergines, artichokes, and onions, surrounded by a border of twig lattice.

A native winged elm tree shades the stone terrace behind the cottage where Ryan often hosts outdoor entertainments. An iron candelabra, now available in a line of garden accessories based on pieces he has designed or collected, adds elegance to the outdoor room bordered by one of the original greenhouses.

ABOVE: *All of the roses in the garden are antique varieties grown on their own rootstock. Their cascading blooms create a romantic atmosphere reminiscent of English cottage gardens, while lead ornaments and miniature temples contribute a more formal elegance.*
OPPOSITE: *Ryan designed a rustic framework of locust timbers to enclose a long garden room furnished with geometric topiary and pruned hedges. Even in winter, when the climbing roses covering the locust beams die back, the garden's boxwoods issue an invitation to enter this quiet green bower.*

Transplanting Time

HIGHLANDS, NORTH CAROLINA

The Blue Ridge Mountain home of Atlantans Mose and Teri Bond seems always to have stood in the wooded valley where it overlooks a field of grass and wildflowers. But in truth, its foundation was laid one hundred and fifty miles away by a planter from Virginia who sought his fortune on the Georgia frontier. Claiming his land grant in the late eighteenth century, Redmond Thornton built a sturdy two-room caretaker's house with a brick foundation tall enough to shelter livestock from Creek Indian raids. Prospering despite the challenges of frontier living, the pioneer family grew and, in 1820, Thornton's eldest son took over the house, more than doubling its size. From the time that Teri's ancestors moved into the house in the mid-nineteenth century up until the present, few other changes were made.

Teri's earliest memories of the farmhouse date from the 1950s, when she visited four great-aunts who lived there in old-fashioned Southern style. "Those were very happy days," she says, recalling the sound of a piano playing, delicious meals prepared in the old kitchen house, and gardens of vegetables, flowers, and fruit trees. Even after the last of the great-aunts left, Teri continued to visit. One day, she discovered that the living room mantel had been pried off the wall and left in the hallway by architectural scavengers. "I was jarred into action to save the house for future generations," she says, "but the prospect of moving it to a more accessible location was daunting."

Fortunately, she had the support of her husband, Mose, a longtime member of the Georgia Trust for Historic Preservation, and their friend, architect and preservationist Norman Askins. "When I showed Norman the house and asked if I should rescue it, he told me I didn't have a choice," she says. "I had to." With his help, she found the perfect site in Highlands, North Carolina, and soon after, a team of builders, house

The plain Georgia huntboard in the center hall is similar to what the original occupants of the late eighteenth-century farmhouse might have placed inside their front door. While rustic Georgia pottery jugs might also have been there for centuries, an antique iron doorstop in the shape of a dog reveals the present-day residents' passion for Jack Russell terriers.

movers, and Amish carpenters began the arduous process of relocating and reassembling the house. Dismantling every board, beam, and brick, the workers coded them with numbers, letters, and colors. Only the staircase was moved intact—and it failed inspection three times before passing because it's antiquated tread-to-riser ratio was so far removed from modern ones.

Norman changed little after the house was reassembled, only adding a bathroom and butler's pantry on the ground floor, borrowing space from the attic for two upstairs bathrooms, and replacing the brick foundation with local stone. Constructed with pine beams and boards like those originally used, his additions are nearly indistinguishable from the house's earliest rooms. All of the original material remains intact, right down to the original buttermilk paint— faded pink in the center hall, bluish gray in the living room, and vestiges of green in the dining room, where newer layers of paint were scraped away.

Once the restoration and remodeling was complete, Teri decorated the house in typical farmhouse style. "Houses like these were never furnished

Built in the late eighteenth century, Teri and Mose Bond's house began as a rustic two-room farm overseer's house on the Georgia frontier. Once painted white, the house's original pine siding has weathered to a natural shade of grayish brown and its original brick foundation has been replaced by local fieldstone that anchors it to its new location.

in a fancy way," says Teri, who used a mix of family heirlooms and simple country furnishings. Although many pieces were purchased from antiques stores and flea markets, every room has at least one object rich in family lore. One of these is the red, pink, and yellow braided rug that creates a bright spot of color in the living room. Made by Teri's mother in anticipation of her birth, it adds to the feeling that generations of families have lived in and loved one another in this house.

More family antiques decorate the dining room, where a Southern pine table with many leaves stretches long enough to seat fourteen during family gatherings. Pink china vases that belonged to Teri's grandmother garnish the mantel and pieces of cut glass and silver passed down through the years stand on a butler's table. Teri's collection of nineteenth-century chairs surrounds the table and lines the walls. Although

they are all painted black, some have seats of cane and others, rush or leather, and few have matching shapes. "I never use identical chairs around a table," says Teri.

Faded kilim rugs cover many floors in the house, combined with antique Southern textiles, including appliqué, colorful chenille embroidery, and hand-sewn quilts. In the master bedroom, a quilt inherited by Mose hangs above the bed—a four-poster made for Teri on her twenty-first birthday of wood from her great-grandmother's house. A painted screen that stands before the fireplace depicts a woman sitting at a spinning wheel in a frontier cabin home. "I remember sitting and looking at that fire screen when I was a child," Teri reminisces. "There is a picture hanging on the wall of the painted room that could be a portrait of my full-blooded Creek Indian great-great-grandmother."

Now Teri and Mose are making their own memories in the house, hosting gatherings with new generations, planting a garden with pass-along plants from friends and neighbors, and starting a grove of serviceberry trees. "When our grandchildren visit, they have the same experiences we had growing up—biking, swimming, and catching tadpoles," says Teri. When she is alone in the house, Teri feels a deep connection not only to the house's past, but also to the new place where it stands. "I love to sit quietly on the front steps and pay attention," she says, "listening to the sounds of wildlife and watching the clouds float by."

OPPOSITE, FAR LEFT: *Sunlight shines through the antique panes of original double-sash windows, illuminating branches of bittersweet arranged in bell jars mounted on wrought-iron plant stands.* OPPOSITE, LEFT: *Old apothecary jars from Teri's father's pharmacy and miniature chests of drawers made as samples by a nineteenth-century cabinetmaker stand on the hall table.* ABOVE: *A charmingly primitive piece of nineteenth-century appliqué hangs on the dining room walls along with other antique textiles.*

The pine-plank walls of the living room are still covered with original buttermilk paint, once a brighter shade of blue. Comfortably furnished with upholstered chairs and a Victorian sofa slipcovered in ticking, the living room is decorated with American antiques, including a decoupage chest and rocking chair.

ABOVE: *Candles flickering from candelabras and a pair of antique English lusters on the sideboard are often the only illumination in the dining room. Pieces of silver and cut glass handed down through Teri's family stand on a butler's table beneath a framed chenille-work textile depicting a cardinal.* OPPOSITE: *Architect Norman Askins scraped away several layers of paint with a penknife to expose a patch of the dining room's original shade of green. Once the rest of the walls were scraped and sanded, vestiges of old paint created a patina that speaks of time's passage.*

ABOVE: *Antique kilims and family quilts add color and pattern to the master bedroom. A twenty-first birthday gift to Teri, the bed was made by a Greene County craftsman of wood salvaged from a family home. The Empire shelf clock standing on the simple mantel was passed down through Mose's family.* OPPOSITE: *Twelve-inch-wide boards cut from virgin pine cover the walls and ceilings of the old farmhouse. While the siding of the original hallway has always been left in its natural, unfinished state, original buttermilk paint adds a rosy glow to the walls of the hall extension added in the early nineteenth century.*

Beach Dreams

SULLIVAN'S ISLAND, SOUTH CAROLINA

The Sullivan's Island home of Hartley and Ashley Cooper brings together the beach memories of four different people. Ashley, who grew up in nearby Charleston, recalls halcyon days at his grandparents' cottage on the island next door. Hartley remembers equally happy childhood times at her family's beach house on Florida's Gulf Coast. Interior designer Amelia Handegan, who has decorated multiple beach houses in the area, brought her familiarity and fondness of South Carolina's coastal cottages to the project. And Beau Clowney, the designer of the house's restoration and expansion, spent years studying the island's vernacular architecture.

When the Coopers began searching for a place to raise their family, Hartley's first choice was downtown Charleston. But Ashley wanted their children to grow up in the relaxed island setting and close-knit community he knew as a child. "Sullivan's Island was—and still is—a place where kids ride their bikes downtown to buy ice cream, families relax at the beach, and neighbors get together every day," he says. "The door was always open at my grandparents' cottage with friends coming and going, and I wanted the same thing for my children." Beguiled by this vision, Hartley agreed, and before long, the couple was living in a 1901 Sullivan's Island cottage with their first child.

With the birth of a second child, the Coopers outgrew the small house and turned to Beau for help expanding it. "We knew he had always respected the historic character of the island and captured its vernacular style," says Hartley. After suggesting ways to adapt their current home, Beau showed them a cottage he had already restored and expanded. "It was the first time my husband ever walked through a house and said 'I love

The original green paint of the front porch ceiling remains, just one of the many old-fashioned elements of this Sullivan's Island beach house.

ABOVE: *With a low hipped roof and a wraparound porch that connects the main part of the house to a small pavilion-like structure, this circa 1890 beach cottage is a classic example of Sullivan's Island vernacular style. Although the addition designed by Beau Clowney more than doubles the original cottage's size, it is nearly invisible from the street.* OPPOSITE: *Landscape architect Sheila Wertimer planted sabal palms in front of a ligustrum hedge to create a sense of enclosure along the outer edge of the pool terrace. The hipped roof and white-painted board walls of a small storage pavilion visually unite it with the original cottage.*

this place,'" Hartley recalls. "He loved the old pine, the high ceilings, everything down to the push-button light switches that reminded him of his mother's childhood home in Charleston."

The project began with the restoration of the original late nineteenth-century cottage—a small two-story building with an attached structure Beau describes as a classic Sullivan's Island pavilion. From the unfinished pine walls and ceilings of the ground-floor rooms to the painted shiplap siding in the bedrooms above, Beau preserved the cottage's original materials. Reorienting the stairs to accentuate the vista through the house to the garden beyond, he captured the airy feel of traditional Southern center-hall houses. And in the pavilion, where he opened the ceiling up to the beams of its pyramidal roof, he created a room that, though modern in volume, is old-fashioned in material and style.

As he drew plans for the addition, Beau took cues from the vernacular architecture of Sullivan's Island. "There is a long history here of houses that

Well known for her love of color, sensual textures, exotic textiles, and juxtapositions of antique and modern styles, interior designer Amelia Handegan combines these in a way that never competes with the house's low-key coastal style. "I love the integrity of these old houses," says Amelia, who decorated the front sitting room with a triptych by Timothy McDowell, mid-century chairs, and a faded antique Oushak that softens its pine surfaces.

evolved over time as their inhabitants moved nearby outbuildings and linked them to the main dwelling," he explains. Beau emulated such houses by dividing the addition into two distinct structures joined by slender, light-filled corridors. These transparent connectors include a hallway with French windows on one side and a bar resembling a butler's pantry on the other that leads from the original cottage to a multipurpose living area.

In this new wing, Beau combined painted shiplap walls and heart-pine floors with a modern, open floor plan. By creating strong focal points on either end of the room, the Coopers' interior designer gave both living and dining areas individual character. Covering one wall of the dining room with a mural of swimmers inspired by the paintings of Henri Matisse, Amelia transformed the entire room into a work of art. In the

living room, a pair of slipcovered sofas defines a seating area around a mantel of rough-hewn reclaimed pine. Concealing a television above the fireplace, the bold markings of two Pygmy drawings add more visual impact.

At the far end of this long room, a passageway lined with windows does double duty as a breakfast room, which is one of the family's favorite spots. "We eat most meals here, the children do art projects on the table, and in the afternoon, I can work and watch them swim in the pool," says Hartley. Aware of the young family's casual, busy lifestyle, Amelia decorated the house with that in mind. Combining the comfort and practicality of slipcovers and hemp rugs with a sophisticated selection of art, antiques, and textiles, she created an environment that satisfies the needs of both adults and children.

"It was clear that the interior design needed to be pared down but lively," says Amelia, who at Hartley's request integrated shades of orange and coral as well as a few mid-twentieth-century pieces. Although unexpected, exotic elements like the entrance hall's Oushak rug and antique Chinese lute table are surprisingly compatible with the house's rustic

OPPOSITE, FAR LEFT: *Beau lined cabinets in the butler's pantry–style bar with painted beadboard paneling and designed mullioned glass doors reminiscent of Southern cottage-style windows.* OPPOSITE, LEFT: *Luminous blue ceramics and antique coral call to mind the beach house's seaside setting.* ABOVE: *Amelia commissioned Kristin Bunting to paint a mural inspired by Matisse's paintings of swimmers for the dining room.* PAGES 104–105: *The mural gives a strong sense of character to the dining room, which, with no partition wall separating it from the adjoining living room, could have easily lacked definition. Glass globe lights that hang at random heights in front of the mural resemble bubbles in an imaginary sea.*

ABOVE: *Two sofas slipcovered with white cotton define the boundaries of the open-plan living room's sitting area. A brick fire surround, rustic pine mantel, Pygmy drawings on bark paper, and chairs upholstered in figured cotton linen bring pattern and texture into the space. "I knew the interior had to be simple, but not at the expense of sophistication," says Amelia.* OPPOSITE: *Beau designed what he calls "glass connectors" to join the three parts of the house. This hallway, which also serves as a breakfast room, links the kitchen with the bedroom wing. Windows overlooking a garden on one side and pool terrace on the other also forge a connection between the room's interior and the lush coastal setting.*

materials and simple details. Such infusions of unexpected color and pattern, including the breakfast room's tangerine-colored chairs and master bedroom's Pakistani wedding shawl, accent every room. Yet the overall feeling of the interior design balances dynamic energy with calm.

Wrapped around a pool courtyard designed by landscape architect Sheila Wertimer, the entire house is suffused with light and surrounded by semitropical verdure. "One of the things I like about the island's old houses is the way they pay homage to the natural beauty around them," says Ashley. "They never dominate." Respecting the island's native landscape, preserving and updating its vernacular architecture, and perpetuating its oldfashioned lifestyle, the Coopers' house offers a new chapter in the story of a place where the old way of life is still intact.

Amelia purchased the Pakistani wedding shawl hanging in the master bedroom on a recent trip to India. Combined with more traditional furniture, including antique French chests of drawers and a four-poster bed, it creates an environment that is both familiar and exotic. "I love weaving together diverse elements to create a thread of continuity," Amelia says. "Nothing shouts and everything nestles together."

SIMPLY *Elegant*

Elegance can be intimidating, especially when houses with ornate architectural detail are furnished in equally opulent style. If there is no place for the eye to rest or the body to relax, highly decorated rooms can impress without providing comfort. Simply elegant houses are different. Intended to foster a sense of ease, they offer quiet settings within which more decorative details provide unanticipated moments of delight. Rooms that combine the graceful lines of Louis XV chairs with uncomplicated curtains or colorful Middle Eastern carpets with slipcovered sofas balance pattern, color, and intricate shapes with their opposites. In a Florida beach house, refined bronze end tables share space on a grass rug with a driftwood lamp, taking seaside style up a notch. And in an urban cottage, walls and ceilings of painted beadboard downplay surprising Gothic-style details. Balance lies at the heart of simply elegant style, creating rooms with an infectious sense of harmony.

A chalky white glaze softens the ornate gilt frame of a nineteenth-century mirror hanging in lighting designer Julie Neill's New Orleans double-shotgun house. Weathered vestiges of paint on a wooden lamp made from a salvaged architectural ornament contrast with the gleaming gold bands and crystal pendants of a chandelier reflected in the mirror.

Collecting Memories

SAVANNAH, GEORGIA

Interior designer Lynn Morgan grew up in a Regency-style house in a turn-of-the-nineteenth-century suburb of Savannah, Georgia. Built by William Gordon Lowe, grandson of Girl Scouts founder Juliette Gordon Lowe, the house was an exact replica of his grandmother's Savannah birthplace. When Lynn remembers childhood, she recalls the house's elegant rooms decorated in classic Southern style with antiques and floral chintz. Her husband, Jeff, in contrast, spent his youth in New England in a house filled with the mid-century modern furniture that his more fashion-forward parents preferred.

A lifetime later, the couple remains true to their earliest memories, dividing time between a New York City high-rise apartment with glass walls and contemporary decor and a Greek Revival townhouse on one of Savannah's quaintest brick-paved streets. While their Manhattan home is purely modern in look, the couple's Savannah retreat offers a synthesis of new and traditional styles. It also reflects another design influence—Lynn and Jeff's shared love of the tropical colors and relaxed lifestyle of the Virgin Islands.

When his father retired early and moved to Saint Croix, Jeff began visiting the island. Later, his wife and children joined him, traveling from the Connecticut farmhouse where they raised their children to the Virgin Islands several times a year. Before long, hints of the tropics began appearing in their New England home—prints and paintings of blue water; clusters of white coral; and pottery, rugs, and tableware in shades of turquoise and green. "The Virgin Islands are so vibrant," says Jeff. "They made a big impression on us in terms of color and design."

This influence finds full expression in the 1865 Savannah townhouse Lynn and Jeff bought as an escape from New York nine years ago. "You can get to Savannah almost as quickly as to the Hamptons, leave

Like many of Savannah's nineteenth-century residences, the Morgans' 1865 townhouse is an attached dwelling with steep stairs that ascend to a raised first floor. Dating from the days before air-conditioning and electric lighting, this design brought more light and air into the principal rooms and protected them from floodwaters.

your worries behind, and spend a restorative weekend of bicycling and strolling in a beautiful old city," says Jeff, mentioning just a few reasons why they chose to put down new roots in Lynn's old hometown. When they began hunting for a second home there, their primary requirements were spacious rooms, plentiful light, and well-preserved architectural details. With tall windows, high ceilings, and handsome Greek Revival moldings, the mid-nineteenth-century townhouse on West Jones Street met most of their criteria. But, Lynn recalls, "Everything was painted brown or maroon and the blinds hadn't been opened to sunlight in years."

As soon as the Morgans purchased the house, they began a restoration that was more cosmetic than structural in nature. "Mostly, it was about bringing the house back to life," says Lynn, who was the decorating editor of *House & Garden* magazine in the 1970s and '80s. Lightening the walls, removing heavy curtains, and inviting a friend, decorative painter Valerie Wall, to embellish the floors, Lynn created a fresh, modern look within the rooms' traditional architecture. A turquoise metal watering can stands at the top of the steep stairs leading to the brick townhouse's front door—the first indication that the interior might not conform entirely to formal Savannah style. This suggestion is confirmed the moment the front door opens to an entrance hall that is simultaneously fresh and traditional in appearance. Period-style wainscoting covers the walls, a historical detail added by the Morgans to complement the house's original Greek Revival moldings. But the dynamic border of blue-and-khaki-colored stripes painted around the floor's perimeter and a striped runner in similar tones prove that modern-day tastes have arrived.

In the adjoining parlor, the pale blue upholstery of Louis XVI chairs, turquoise-painted French bistro tables, and natural grass matting repeats the hall's color scheme. Inspired by the sand and sea of Saint Croix, the palette is cool, casual, and elegant all at once. Louvered blinds do little to block the light that floods the airy space, and pocket doors invite sunlight into the adjoining dining room, which, located in the center of the townhouse, has no windows of its own. In this room, brightly upholstered chairs surround a country Swedish table that once stood in the Morgans' Connecticut kitchen. "Some people might say the table is not dressy enough for a Savannah townhouse," says Lynn, "but we love its simplicity." Although the tufted chairs were meant to add formality, their fanciful silhouettes, painted legs, and vivid green upholstery are far from serious. The turquoise-and-blue-striped rug, which Lynn says, "brings the beach to town," is equally lighthearted.

OPPOSITE: *In the entrance hall, interior designer Lynn Morgan combined an ornate mirror inherited from her grandfather with a simple Swedish table.* PAGES 116–117: *Unlike the heavy draperies favored in traditional Savannah interiors, white louvered shutters reveal the living room's Greek Revival moldings and fill the space with light. Within the room's pale palette, a print from David Hockney's pool series recalls the azure shades of the Caribbean Sea.*

"Savannah is filled with brick, cobblestone, and dark green foliage," says Jeff. "It's nice to come home to a place with vibrant color."

While Lynn took charge of the interior design, the furnishing of the courtyard was supervised by Jeff, an importer of special papers with an equally good eye for design. "I wanted to find a French wrought-iron garden table, but that's not easy in Savannah," he says. Instead, with the help of local antiques dealer Alex Raskin, Jeff found a table cast in Atlanta in the 1920s accompanied by a set of uncomfortable iron chairs. Leaving the chairs behind, he bought the table and set it in the center of the garden, where jasmine-covered walls, boxwood hedges, a magnolia tree, and camellias offer fragrance, shade, and greenery year-round.

Once Jeff acquired a foursome of springy 1950s garden chairs at auction, the garden was finally ready for company. "They're so whimsical and the white paint provides a nice contrast to the foliage," says Jeff. When the Morgans are in town, Lynn's touring bike, a gift from Jeff in her favorite shade of blue, stands in the courtyard ready for a spin. "Wherever I am, these are the colors that make me happy," says Lynn. Summing up the philosophy that has shaped the design of all the homes she and Jeff have shared, she explains, "If you love something, you'll be true to it forever."

ABOVE: *Over the years, Lynn has collected napkins, glassware, and plates that she loves to combine in colorful table settings. Topped with sea urchin votives, pearly baubles, bubble vases, and a coral centerpiece, a painted Swedish table assumes a beachy personality.*
OPPOSITE: *A French pier mirror and antique chandelier are the only suggestions of Savannah-style formality in a dining room where whimsical upholstered chairs surround an antique country Swedish table.*

ABOVE: *The master bedroom opens through French doors to a balcony-like sitting room overlooking the courtyard garden. The doors' translucent lower panes provide privacy at night without blocking light by day. Lynn kept the design of the room as simple as possible in order to let architectural details, including the Greek Revival door surrounds and mantel, speak clearly.* OPPOSITE: *When the Morgans purchased the house, this sunny room's walls were covered with patterned metallic wallpaper from the 1950s. Redecorating the room in pale blue and white, Lynn created a serene retreat. "It's a wonderful place I can call my own," she says.* PAGES 122–123: *A low boxwood hedge and brick border create a graceful circular terrace inside the townhouse's small courtyard. Dense vines and flowering trees provide a cool, fragrant setting for outdoor cocktail parties and dinners around the cast-iron table made in Atlanta in the 1920s.*

Creole Simplicity

NEW ROADS, LOUISIANA

The unpretentious beauty of the Creole plantation houses that haunt Louisiana's bayous and riversides is rooted in nature, steeped in history, and mellowed by the passage of centuries. Shaped by the climate, they were shaded by wide hipped roofs and generous porches to protect their interiors from the region's intense sun, heat, and frequent rain. Constructed of handmade brick, local cypress, and even Spanish moss, clay, and straw used in a primitive insulation called *bousillage*, they quite literally grew out of their natural settings. Bearing closer resemblance to French West Indian plantation houses than to the Georgian and Federal dwellings found elsewhere in the South, their appearance reflected the cultural isolation of their setting—rural farmlands pioneered by Spanish and French colonial planters who continued to speak their own languages long after Louisiana became an American state.

Like an unbroken thread in an antique tapestry, LeJeune House traces the story of Creole plantation style from the eighteenth century to the present. Although the precise building date of the house in New Roads, Louisiana, is unknown, the 500-acre sugar plantation it graced was established in 1790 by a Frenchman named Francois Samson, who was employed by the Spanish government in power at the time. When the plantation began to thrive, Samson constructed his family's home on a low rise on the banks of the False River—a large lake that was once part of the nearby Mississippi.

Standing beneath the shade of an ancient oak, the house was built in traditional Creole style, with two ground-floor rooms constructed of brick laid between rugged cypress posts. On the second wood-framed story, two more large rooms opened to a deep porch that wrapped all four sides of the house. While the

Watercolors of Paris painted by Richard Gibb's mother, who studied art in France, hang above a simple nineteenth-century sofa upholstered with Scalamandre silk velvet. Unusual transoms added in the nineteenth century that feature muntins in a running-bond brick pattern surmount interior doorways and Creole-style divided glass doors.

sturdy masonry of the ground floor was designed to withstand periodic flooding from the surrounding waters, the second floor's tall ceilings and French doors were intended to offer respite from the sultry climate. Today, this original structure remains, speaking of the past while also reflecting modifications made by the LeJeune family, who purchased the plantation from Samson in the nineteenth century.

As the family grew in number, the plantation prospered, and architectural tastes changed, the new residents expanded and remodeled the house in the Greek Revival style. Replacing the hipped roof with a gabled one, encasing French Colonial–style colonnettes with square pillars, embellishing rooms with classically inspired moldings and mantels, and enclosing side and rear porches to create new rooms, they added stature and refinement to the modest dwelling. When the plantation's prosperity faded, subsequent generations of the LeJeunes made few additional changes.

Present-day residents Randy Harelson and Richard Gibbs had no plans for settling in Louisiana when they found the old plantation house with a "for

When LeJeune House was built in the early 1800s, it was surrounded by a Creole-style wraparound porch with square brick columns below and slender colonnettes above. After the house was remodeled in the Greek Revival style, the traditional French colonial hipped roof was replaced with gables and the colonnettes were encased within tapering wood pillars.

sale" sign. Then living in Florida, they discovered the house while visiting New Roads, where Randy spent summers as a child. Connoisseurs of traditional architecture—Randy is author of *New Roads and Old Rivers: Louisiana's Historic Pointe Coupée Parish* and Richard served as town architect for Florida's Seaside and Rosemary Beach—they were enchanted by the house's beautifully preserved facade. When they toured its interior, they were amazed at the antique quality of the rooms within. "It was evident that the house had been well cared for, never abandoned, and always loved," says Richard. "It had a wonderful, positive energy."

Richard and Randy bought the property five days later. Soon afterward, Randy spent a night in the house, pondering the idea that so many people had been born and had died there. After falling asleep on a makeshift bed, he awoke and looked at his watch. "It was midnight on the button—even the second hand was at twelve," he recalls. "The witching hour, I thought."

In earlier days, the house's kitchen was located in an outbuilding. In the twentieth century, one of the original ground-floor rooms was transformed into a kitchen and informal dining area with partially exposed brick-between-post walls and hand-hewn cypress beams. Reflecting the Creole mix of European and American cultures, an 1854 hand-colored etching depicting Benjamin Franklin in the French court hangs above a primitive Southern jelly cupboard.

Waiting for sounds of restless spirits, instead he felt as though a blanket of peacefulness settled over him. When he left the next day, the tangible sensation of serenity remained.

This quality of calm pervades the cool shadows of ground-floor rooms, where handmade brick, natural stucco, and exposed cypress beams are among the hallmarks of early Creole architecture. Brighter light illuminates the second-floor rooms, in which the restrained ornamentation of Greek Revival pilasters, blind friezes, and coffered ceilings add elegance without ornamental excess. In the parlor, Richard and Randy avoided formal symmetry, creating intimate seating areas with antique chairs, tables, and family pieces. Like their predecessors, they combined American furnishings similar to those readily available from New Orleans with more primitive, locally made pieces. With the

exception of a massive armoire typical to Creole interiors, most of the furniture is small in scale and uncomplicated in design. "LeJeune House is a simple home with quiet grandeur," Randy says. "Even with coffered ceilings and classical moldings, it doesn't show off. Houses with charm never brag."

OPPOSITE: *This ground-floor space served as the house's original dining room. While exposed cypress beams are Creole vestiges, a Greek Revival mantel dates from the remodeling that occurred several decades after the house was built. Purchased in New England, the mahogany table and gondola chairs are similar to American furnishings imported through New Orleans in the nineteenth century.*
ABOVE: *Arranged on a Vieux Paris platter, Meyer lemons grown on the property form a simple table decoration.*

While its stately pilasters and coffered ceiling are Greek Revival in style, the parlor's furniture arrangement recalls Creole residents' practical approach to decoration. With rooms frequently serving multiple purposes—plantation business by day and family life at night—easily moveable, lightweight furniture was favored. "Although they were embellished here and there with luxury items, these houses were not overly grand by today's standards," says Randy.

ABOVE: *In the master bedroom, reproduction toile from Scalamandre features scenes of ships and fishing boats that call to mind the house's riverfront setting. "We always tried to find furniture and materials that were available in the nineteenth century and appropriate to the look and feel of the house," says Richard. The room's French armoire resembles Louisiana-made pieces of the same period.* OPPOSITE: *Deep, wraparound fireplaces are one of the hallmarks of Creole style. Although embellished with a Greek Revival mantel and overmantel, the master bedroom's fireplace still hearkens to French colonial style.*

Harmonic Composition

MONTGOMERY, ALABAMA

Located in a historic neighborhood of Montgomery, Alabama, Richard Norris and Mark Leslie's circa 1915 Colonial Revival house has a formal facade graced by a neoclassical portico and Federal fanlights. The herringbone brick walk and marble front steps suggest that the interior will be equally conventional, but a quick look at the entrance hall immediately dispels this impression. Filled with a surprising array of disparate objects, including a wrought-iron French jardinière, a headless statue of Saint Denis framed by a Gothic panel, and a pair of moose antlers, the room reveals a much more catholic approach to design.

Although the foyer's contents may seem a far cry from traditional Southern style, Richard and Mark are quick to cite the entrance hall at Monticello as a pedigreed historical precedent. Furnished by Thomas Jefferson, that room is a cabinet of curiosities decorated with Indian artifacts, religious art, a great clock, marble-topped tables—and moose antlers. "You can tell that Jefferson was widowed young," Mark says. "No woman would have allowed a room to be decorated like that."

When Richard and Mark first saw their house, it had wall-to-wall carpet, paint, and draperies in the powder-blue shade favored by Jacqueline Kennedy, accented by red toile in the foyer and gold-foil wallpaper in the dining room. Now the house's rooms are painted in subtle shades of brown or beige with moldings to match. This neutral palette creates an unobtrusive backdrop for the sundry treasures Richard and Mark have plundered over the years from childhood homes, European curiosity shops, local antiques stores, and country flea markets. "If you create a quiet setting, then all the objects in a room work together in harmony," says Richard, revealing the influence of architect and interior designer Bobby McAlpine, whose office he manages.

In the entrance hall, the sealskin-colored walls, moldings, and ceiling create a quiet background for a collection of distinctive objects of a variety of materials and styles. The Napoleon III clock, pewter and crystal chandelier, and moose antlers seem unlikely roommates, but within the dusky calm of the foyer, they work together harmoniously.

The virtue of this design philosophy is demonstrated in the long living- and dining-room space, in which there are no matched suites of furniture. In the dining area, a combination of Regency Revival chairs and upholstered ones surrounds a table with a rustic top of reclaimed wood on cabriole legs. "The chairs are a collection of individuals, just like the people who surround our table," says Mark. The author of *Beyond the Pasta*, a book about Italian cuisine and family life, he adds, "I like the idea of this being a family table where you can pull up another chair whenever someone else arrives."

A grand piano stands against one wall of the room, silhouetted against a shell-shaped sounding board salvaged from a church. Opposite, an ornately carved marble mantel added in the 1960s to replace the original Adam-esque one introduces a baroque detail. Although it doesn't really fit the architecture or decor, the current residents couldn't bring themselves to discard the mantel. "I've come to appreciate the artistry of its carving, the beauty of the marble, and the symbolism of the pomegranates, grapes, and acanthus leaves," says Richard.

BELOW: *Mark and Richard enjoy creating table settings with the things they love—transferware plates with historical scenes of Birmingham, Alabama, hand-turned wooden salad bowls, and flowers picked from the garden.* OPPOSITE: *Symmetry adds order to a dining area that includes mid-twentieth-century French consoles, a custom table with reclaimed pine and cabriole legs, and intentionally unmatched chairs. Monochromatic walls and moldings and uncurtained windows modernize the architecture's Colonial Revival details.*

In the seating area, a sofa and unmatched chairs designed by McAlpine surround a 1960s mirrored table from Richard's childhood home. Covering one wall of the space, a large decorative screen hand-painted by Montgomery artist David Braly combines elements that appeal to both residents. While cornstalks remind Mark of his Midwestern roots, a pattern of Gothic tracery draws from the ecclesiastical architecture beloved by Richard. "We don't really decorate," explains Mark. "We just surround ourselves with things we love."

Converting the original dining room into a spacious kitchen was the only major change Mark and Richard made to the house. "Our goal was to retain vestiges of the room's previous incarnation in the new design," says Richard, who found ways to modernize the room while still honoring its more formal past. Crowned by a gilt mirror, the large stove looks a bit like a sideboard. Recessed into the cabinetry, the refrigerator resembles a china closet. An oval island centered beneath an ornate bronze light fixture reminds the residents of their predecessor's dining table and chandelier.

In the master bedroom upstairs, the furnishings recount a more personal past, reminding their owners of different times in their lives. The chrome and leather Wassily chairs that form a sitting area were the first pieces of furniture Richard purchased after graduating from Auburn University. Antique pressed seaweed specimens, coral, and a starfish came from the home Richard and Mark shared in Seagrove, Florida. And the rustic headboard made of wood salvaged from an old stable is a souvenir from a joint antiquing foray in rural Alabama.

Most of the time, Mark and Richard pick out their furniture and decorative objects together, but in some cases, one or the other smuggles in a piece in the form of a gift, hoping it will find a permanent place. One Christmas, Mark gave an illuminated figure of a choirboy to Richard, who is a real-life chorister. The piece adds a lighthearted touch to a masculine dressing room occupied by three massive antique wardrobes. "There is a poetry that comes from bringing together things that you love," says Richard, "as long as you give them space to breathe."

PAGES 140–141: *Walls and moldings are painted an identical shade of beige in the living and dining room. "When this is done, objects in a room become more important because the architecture isn't upstaging them," says Richard. Throughout the space, larger objects with simple shapes, like the sounding board behind the piano and cabriole-legged dining table, balance intricate pieces including a Gothic Revival chair.* OPPOSITE: *A chandelier made by joining two antique bronze sconces, heavy crown molding, and elegant dado panels hint at the kitchen's origins as a dining room. The remainder of the room's contents, including the marble-topped island and stainless-steel appliances, are simpler and more utilitarian.*

ABOVE: *Constructed from wide hand-hewn pine boards that might once have been part of an old stable, the headboard contributes a primitive element to the master bedroom's sophisticated, modern decor.* OPPOSITE: *In the master bedroom's sitting area, the sleek modernism of Wassily chairs and an Eames table contrast with the organic textures of a jute rug and pressed seaweed specimens displayed above tambour demilune consoles designed by Richard.*

Richard designed a romantic rose-and-boxwood parterre garden encircled by jasmine-covered walls behind the house. Following the property's sloping terrain, it has the slightly off-kilter charm of an old English garden.

Cottage Gothic

ATLANTA, GEORGIA

When Steve and Louise Moreland purchased a house in a picturesque neighborhood in Atlanta, Georgia, they expected to renovate it, but not to rebuild entirely. What first attracted them to the 1934 residence was its winningly simple style and modest scale, ideal for a couple whose children had grown and moved to other parts of the world. When they discovered irreversible termite and water damage, however, they knew they had to tear it down and start from scratch, building a new house with the same congenial spirit as the one it replaced.

With dark brown shingles and crisp white trim, the new cottage differs in appearance from the original white frame house, but still perfectly complements the turn-of-the-twentieth-century neighborhood streetscape. Designed by architect Norman Askins, it is unaffected in style, but dressed up a bit with architectural detail. "The house needed to be full of charm, but not at the expense of elegance and grace," the architect says. The Morelands' interior designer Jackye Lanham agrees: "Steve and Louise have always loved houses that combine charm with sophistication."

There are many things that make a house charming—intimate scale, unpretentious design, quirky details, and a sense of having been lived in and loved. The way Norman tucked the front door beneath an alcove on the side of the cottage instead of its facade is just one of the dwelling's engaging features. Rather than opening into a spacious entrance hall, the door leads to a small foyer from which the kitchen and dining room are both visible. "We threw out all preconceived notions about the archetypal Southern house

The informal cottage style of the dining room's painted beadboard ceiling balances the refinement of the staircase's graceful banister and demi-lune window. A traditional arrangement of chairs flanking an antique chest of drawers gives this side of the dual-purpose room the appearance of a classic Southern stair hall.

ABOVE: *Designed by architect Norman Askins, Steve and Louise Morelands' house captures the charm of Atlanta's early twentieth-century cottages with an inviting porch, windows in a variety of sizes and shapes, and multiple gables, setbacks, and bays.* OPPOSITE: *A gate with custom-made iron strap hinges and a gas lantern opens to a small side court leading to the cottage's front door. While the original entrance opened directly from the front porch into the living room, this sidelong sequence creates a more romantic, roundabout approach.*

with a grand stair hall and large entertaining rooms," Norman explains. "Every inch counted, so the rooms had to flow into each other and some even needed to serve two functions."

The most inventive of these dual-purpose areas is the dining room, which also serves as a stair hall. To accentuate the staircase rather than play it down, Norman endowed it with a graceful handrail and a demilune window. By centering a heavy ceiling beam directly above the dining room table, he emphasized the room's other function just as strongly. Hanging a crystal chandelier from the beam and surrounding the table with chairs dressed in pretty white skirts, Jackye transformed the space into an elegant dining room.

This small room also serves as a passageway from the foyer to the living room. Like most of the house's interior, the living room's walls are paneled with painted poplar beadboard that lends an informal Southern style. But the recessed shelves that flank the fireplace introduce a much more sophisticated aesthetic inspired by medieval English design. "The tall, skinny niches just begged for Gothic arches," says Norman, who also added Gothic details to door and window mullions, the den's bookcase, and even

Serving an unusual pair of functions, the combined dining room and stair hall has a graceful staircase on one side and an elegant dining bay on the other. Plentiful windows in a variety of shapes and styles bring light into rooms that flow easily from one to the next.

ABOVE: *Concealed within a beadboard wall, a door decorated with antique maritime paintings leads from the library to a laundry room. An Empire chair from Louise's 1809 family farmhouse in Delaware and an eighteenth-century Virginia corner cupboard are among the room's antique furnishings.* OPPOSITE: *"If everything dates from the same period or reflects a certain trend, rooms can be boring," says interior designer Jackye Lanham, who prefers interiors reflecting a lifetime of travel and collecting. In the Morelands' living room, Jackye combined a family portrait, French papier-mâché pole screens, circa 1810, and an English traveler's trunk.*

bathrooms. "The style of the house went from simple cottage to Gothic," says Louise, who initially had reservations about this twist. "I wasn't sure the two ideas worked together." But soon she recognized how the Gothic shapes added whimsy to the house's rooms and prevented them from feeling cramped or boxy. Before long, Steve even purchased a Gothic Revival chair that echoed the decorative trim of the den's bookcase.

This marriage of informal American and traditional English styles proved a perfect setting for the Morelands' collection of antique furniture and rustic artifacts. Collectors since the early days of their marriage, they began by purchasing Southern furniture, including an eighteenth-century corner cabinet from Virginia. Louise also inherited several pieces from an 1809 farmhouse in Delaware, where she spent many childhood summers. Heirlooms from the family home, including the portrait above the living room mantel, recall memories and add character to the rooms.

Contrasting the dark finish of antiques with natural tones and textures of linen, gauze, and sisal matting, Jackye created an atmosphere she describes as "casually fancy." To unify the cottage's rooms visually, she chose a soft, creamy palette for both paint and upholstery. Only the master bedroom at the back of the house departs from the neutral color scheme. With pale blue walls and soft sage-colored accents, the room seems to converse more with the tiny garden behind it than with the rest of the house.

Casement windows open from the bedroom to a handkerchief-size lawn that is transformed into an intimate outdoor room by the tall, curved Tennessee fieldstone retaining wall that encloses one end. Steve, who collaborated closely with Norman, dreamed up the idea of putting a door to nowhere in the center of the wall. With iron strap hinges and a leaded-glass window, it promises to lead to a tunnel, or a maze, or a secret garden, but instead opens to a small tool room. A folly known only to a few, it adds the finishing touch to the cottage's fanciful charm.

Although the bar area serves as a transitional space between the foyer and library, a pyramidal ceiling with chevron paneling and a Tudor arch gives it stature. To emphasize the small room's height, Jackye selected a glass lantern that casts light upward onto the ceiling. Concealed cabinets and drawers prevent the well-equipped bar from appearing cluttered. The Morelands purchased the painting of a woman by artist A. Russo when they lived on Sea Island, Georgia, in an early twentieth-century cottage restored by Norman.

ABOVE: *Soon after the Morelands married, they commissioned this reproduction bed with tall, slender mahogany posts. Louise purchased the eighteenth-century Scottish trunk at its foot because it reminded her of one her parents owned.* OPPOSITE: *Working with landscape architect Richard Anderson, Norman and Steve designed a curved Tennessee fieldstone wall to enclose the back lawn. Although the lawn is small, an arched doorway set into the stone masonry suggests that another garden room lies beyond the retaining wall.*

Lakeside Reverie

LAKE MARTIN, ALABAMA

Located on the banks of Lake Martin, surrounded by Alabama's piney woods and rural farmland, this retreat combines both rustic charm and urbane style. With beams and trusses of reclaimed barn wood, a double fireplace with a European-inspired chimney breast, and antique oak floors with a modern gray glaze, it reflects both the pastoral longings and worldly sophistication of its residents. "My clients wanted the house to feel like it belonged in the country," says interior designer Paige Schnell of Tracery Interiors, "but they wanted it to have an elegant flair."

The house overlooks the lake with a wall of windows framed out with huge beams of rough-hewn wood. More heavy beams and trusses and a barn-wood ceiling recall the architecture of the region's farm buildings, uniting the interior with the surrounding countryside. But the massive double fireplace that divides the house's long great room into two parts references an entirely different past. With graceful curves and handsome moldings, it recalls the forms of stately French fire surrounds, adding refinement to the space.

The trumeau mirror hanging above the mantel and the living room area's urn-shaped lamps are equally Old World in style. The remaining contents of the open-plan space, however, fall mostly into the modern camp. Even the white-painted pine walls that resemble traditional tongue-and-groove paneling have an up-to-date look. "The extra long grooves between the tongues give the walls a clean, linear appearance," Paige explains.

Throughout the house, the interior designer juxtaposed furnishings with clean, contemporary lines and materials against more organic pieces. A French table made of reclaimed wood stands between two sofas upholstered in crisp white linen. One of the sofas faces the fireplace, where armchairs with equally contemporary silhouettes flank the chimney breast. The other sofa provides seating in the breakfast area, where aluminum Windsor-style chairs encircle a primitive table made of reclaimed oak.

The straight lines of tongue-and-groove-style paneling set off the intricate patterns of an antique carved chest and an Oushak runner. Instead of using canned lights in the hall, interior designer Paige Schnell of Tracery Interiors chose antique iron lanterns.

ABOVE: *Although the materials of the dining area vary widely, from the fieldstone of a rugged pier to white linen slipcovers, the chandelier's gesso and gilt, and aluminum floor lamps, a unifying palette of ivory, beige, and gray bring them into harmony.* OPPOSITE: *Paige opted for painted wood walls and glazed oak floors in this Alabama lake house. Combined with beams and trusses of weathered barn wood, the bright, reflective surfaces provide the ideal backdrop for furnishings that range in style from reclaimed wood tables to contemporary upholstered sofas and chairs.*

A fieldstone pier forms a rugged wall at one end of the dining area, where a table of glazed antique wood complements the grisaille oak floors. Two unmatched sets of chairs surround the table—new chairs slip-covered in white linen and antique Italian ones with carved oak arms. With tall, square backs upholstered in a contemporary pattern and white faux-leather seats, the nineteenth-century chairs appear more modern than antique. Completing the dining area's time-less style, an antique chandelier of gessoed wood, iron, and gilt hangs above the table and stainless-steel floor lamps stand nearby.

Designed for a family of six plus plenty of weekend guests, the house has five bedrooms on the second floor. With tall, mullioned win-dows, painted wood walls and ceilings, and jute rugs, these rooms are light, bright, and informal in style. Decorating them in shades of white, khaki, burlap, and beige, the interior designer only occasionally added accents of color—dark blue in the boys' bedroom, pale aqua in an upstairs hall, a hint of pink in a bedroom for the family's daughters.

The brightest of the bedrooms is a small corner guest room, where four pairs of casement windows frame views of the lake. A soft, white cotton duvet cover and matching bolster transform the bed into an invit-ing nest. The room's unmatched lamps, vintage metal table with vestiges of paint, and old-fashioned bed are reminiscent of the unpretentious decoration of simple country homes.

ABOVE: *Open shelving with brackets reminiscent of Victorian jigsaw work adds antique detail to a kitchen with marble countertops and stainless-steel appliances more in keeping with modern tastes.* OPPOSITE: *In the butler's pantry, a library ladder provides easy access to upper cabinets with cold-rolled steel doors. While the sliding glass doors of the china cabinets recall old-fashioned butler's pantries, drawers with metal pulls, including refrigerator drawers, are modern in style and function.*

ABOVE: *Paige designed the interior finishes of the house, including pine walls with routed grooves that offer a modern interpretation of tongue-and-groove paneling that is a mainstay of Southern vernacular cottages. Modern double blinds hang over the windows of this guest room, one layer sheer and gauzy, the other, opaque—allowing guests to bask in reflected light or dim the room for lazy naps. OPPOSITE: Although the pendant lights are modern in style, their steel shades resemble galvanized aluminum—a more old-fashioned, rural material. Black-and-white family photographs and a vintage chest of drawers with graceful lines make the transitional space feel more like a room than a passageway.*

In the generously sized guest suite, which, with a king-size bed and pair of bunks, is large enough for a family of four, Paige repeats the restful palette. Neutral and serene, the room is dressed up a bit with a pair of French armchairs and a headboard upholstered with paisley linen. But the tongue-and-groove walls and ceiling, jute rug, and burlap-colored curtains keep the decor rooted in the casual style of Southern country cottages. The bedroom opens to a bath chamber with a barn-wood ceiling and a floor of herringbone Carrara marble tiles. Sheer glass curtains and heavy linen drapery soften a tall window that looks across the lake to the wooded bank on its other side. Positioned in front of the window, a long porcelain tub with European-style fixtures provides the perfect lap of luxury from which to enjoy view. "If you're going to put a bathtub by a window, this is the place to do it," says Paige.

Poised on a point of land with water on three sides, the house seems to exist in a time and place all its own. Combining the rustic charm of the rural South with urbane details, Paige created a getaway for clients who want to escape from the city without leaving civilization behind. Elegant, elemental, and ethereal, it is, in the designer's words, "a very romantic retreat."

A restorative retreat that is nearly as large as the master bedroom, the guest suite has polished details that dress up its neutral palette and natural materials. Crisp white trim with buttons on natural linen draperies, the graceful headboard's white paisley and piping, and a pair of Louis XVI armchairs add elegance to the room without overwhelming its restful mood.

Coastal Cloister

ROSEMARY BEACH, FLORIDA

When Rosemary Beach was founded on the Florida Panhandle coast in 1995, its developers chose the architecture of the Dutch West Indies as their aesthetic guide. Although an anomaly among the Emerald Coast's old-fashioned beach towns and New Urbanist developments, the romantic style proved ideal for defining a retreat with the charm and intimacy of a remote colonial town. "In colonies, you always find a naive execution of the mother country's architecture," says Bobby McAlpine, who has designed more than a dozen dwellings there inspired by the island style. With white stucco walls and fanciful parapets, these have what he describes as "a wide-eyed innocence," contributing to an environment where a spirit of calm and reverie replaces the unforgiving pace of the outside world.

Like the Dutch colonial houses that inspired it, the home of property developer Stan Benecki and his wife, interior designer Melanie Turner, addresses the street with what Melanie calls "a happy but elegant face." With a white stucco facade, stair-stepped parapet, and wide-open shutters around a large central window, it greets passersby with a friendly expression. But the house also has the introverted nature of the single houses of Charleston, South Carolina, which rarely have front doors opening directly into the house. Instead, the Beneckis' residence is entered discreetly on the side through a gate that leads to a cloisterlike courtyard. "Coming into the courtyard is like walking into a private oasis," says Melanie. "It makes you feel like you can breathe again."

A deep balcony reminiscent of a Charleston side porch juts over the courtyard, creating a welcome band of shade between the house and a sun-dazzled pool terrace. "This is such a Southern way of thinking about shade and how to be comfortable when you are out of doors," Melanie adds. The two entrances to the

With its baroque curves, zigzagging parapet, and exaggerated window, the Rosemary Beach house designed by Bobby McAlpine for Stan Benecki and Melanie Turner Benecki greets the street with a lively expression. Inspired by Dutch West Indian architecture, the house also draws from the single houses of Charleston, South Carolina, with an off-center courtyard entrance and a second-story side porch.

French doors open from the courtyard to a long room that accommodates the house's dining, living, and kitchen areas. Dutch West Indian–inspired cornices crown doorways on either end of the room, contrasting with simple tongue-and-groove paneling. A cozy alcove opens off one side of the long room, offering an intimate alternative to its expansiveness.

ABOVE: *Instead of a coffee table or ottoman, Melanie placed a pair of bronze and leather end tables in front of the sofa to add height and elegance to the seating area. A driftwood lamp from France introduces a typical beach house material in an unexpected way.* OPPOSITE: *A high-backed banquette from the McAlpine Home Collection embraces a dining table at one end of the living space. Paintings commissioned from Cuban artist Ulises Toache resemble windows framing the mysterious natural beauty of the region's saltwater lagoons.*

OPPOSITE: *Bobby designed an overscaled fireplace backed with Roman-style bricks and filled with ceramic cannonballs to warm an intimate alcove. "The feeling of the room is very compressed," says Bobby. "To exacerbate that, the fireplace is big and devouring." With narrow windows and a ceiling several inches lower than the adjoining space, the alcove is a snug retreat for quiet conversations and solitude.* ABOVE: *The driftwood-like appearance of a petrified wood table combined with a fragile branch of coral bring souvenirs of the seaside setting into the house's sophisticatedly simple decor.*

house are located beneath the balcony's shelter, with one pair of French doors opening into the master bedroom and the other into a long room that serves as the house's living, dining, and kitchen areas.

Combining Melanie's artful approach to coastal style with the subtle sophistication of Bobby's architecture, the interior is serene and inviting. Quintessential beach cottage details, including cotton duck slipcovers and tongue-and-groove walls and ceilings, reference the house's seaside location. "I love planking that has a gap between the boards," says the architect, who left a dime-thin space between the planks. "It feels airy and lets the room breathe." With concrete pavers the color of wet sand, sisal rugs, and washable slipcovers, the living area is a beach-friendly place for grown-ups and children with sandy feet and wet bathing suits.

Throughout the house, Melanie found places for shells, clusters of coral, and driftwood without which any beach house is incomplete. But these are incorporated into the design in a way that is never hackneyed or trite. Driftwood comes in the form of a floor lamp from France, shells sit on the living room area's bronze and leather tables, and white coral is displayed on tables of petrified wood that look like broken trunks of trees washed ashore.

ABOVE: *With open shelving and plentiful cabinet space, a scullery room helps keep the adjacent kitchen's countertop clear for cooking and casual meals.* RIGHT: *A cement-topped island is the only boundary between the combined living and dining area and the kitchen. A wall of travertine tile inspired by the tones of oyster shells conceals the scullery room, where the clutter of a busy kitchen is hidden from view.*

At one end of the long communal space, a high-backed banquet designed by Bobby fills a shallow niche, partially surrounding an antique English table that serves a multitude of purposes. "We use it as a dining table, desk, and place for playing games," says Melanie. In the central seating area, a pair of elegant contemporary end tables stands in front of the sofa, tempering the room's relaxed style with a hint of formality. Opening off this area, an alcove just big enough for two matching sofas and a fireplace creates an intimate alternative to the large room's gregarious mood.

"The fireside alcove is very tight and cozy, allowing you to witness the expansive beauty of the room beside it," says Bobby. Playing opposing energies off one another, the architect designed an overscaled fireplace that nearly fills one wall of the compressed room. Also pairing opposites, Melanie juxtaposed luxurious silk velvet bolsters with plain cotton upholstery and a marble fire surround with the rough bark of petrified wood tables. "I wanted to play up the contrast between the casual and the elegant, the masculine and the feminine, the high and the low," she says.

The interior designer also explored the relationship between the house's interior spaces and the coastal landscape surrounding it. In addition to organic objects and materials that literally bring the outdoors inside, three paintings of the region's saltwater lakes hang on the walls. Commissioned from Cuban artist Ulises Toache, the scenes of dark trees reflected by mysterious lagoons seem like portals into a darkly luminous world.

These paintings invite moments of introspection in a space that is otherwise designed for active living, both for the family of four and friends of all ages. Even the kitchen invites communal interaction, divided from the living and dining areas only by a narrow island that serves as a counter for preparing meals, a table for informal dining, and a buffet for entertaining. "When you cook there, its almost like theater," says Melanie, who invites friends and neighbors over for parties almost every night. With all the pantry space, shelving, and appliances hidden in an adjacent scullery, the kitchen is as clean in style and uncluttered as the rest of the living area.

"Bobby is the master of the small house," says Melanie. "There are always places to gather together and others where you can hide away from view." Among these more private retreats, which also include a family room and three second-floor bedrooms, the master bedroom is a serene, cocoonlike place. Enclosed with white-painted wood walls and heavy velvet draperies, the secluded retreat opens up to the bright light of the courtyard when the curtains are pulled aside. "I have lived in many houses," says Melanie, "but this is the one I love the most. It attends to all emotions."

For the master bedroom, Melanie designed velvet curtains with shades ranging from bluish green to silvery rosemary to capture the shifting colors of the Gulf of Mexico.

Princess Palace

NEW ORLEANS, LOUISIANA

New Orleans–based lighting designer Julie Neill loves to combine the antique with the modern, both in the chandeliers she creates and in her Garden District home. "I love to make history modern," she says. "I don't want to live in the past, but I like to remember what comes before and forge a progression from that." In the Victorian double-shotgun house where she resides, this approach to mingling the past and present is embodied not only as a lighthearted lesson in the decorative arts but also as an expression of personal history.

"I grew up in a double-shotgun house just twenty-five blocks uptown from here," says Julie. "All my adult life, I wanted to live in one that was just like it." It was not until Julie's own children were almost grown and Hurricane Katrina blew the roof off the converted grocery store where she lived that Julie found the house she'd been dreaming of. When she discovered the 1880s double shotgun—a narrow house with a front porch and a pair of front doors opening to two long suites of rooms—she knew that she was home. Grafting her grown-up taste for elegant decor upon the familiar floor plan, she also obeyed a post-Katrina impulse to pare down her possessions to just a few favorite things.

In shimmering rooms decorated in tones of pure white and cream, Julie took a giant leap forward from the dark furniture of her childhood home. The adjoining living and dining room, where only the barest hints of lavender and pink details diverge from the white-on-white palette, are the brightest of these. "Some people

When lighting designer Julie Neill found a pair of 1950s lampshades, she put them in her workshop near a bag of white feathers left over from a ball chandelier she had designed. "The feathers asked to jump on them," she says, "so I just let it happen." Julie also designed the French campaign-style-inspired bed with a graceful canopy frame and gilded palm-leaf motif.

say these rooms look like petits fours," says Julie, referring to the little cakes iced in white with tiny pastel swirls and dots. "But to me, the house is like a deep breath of fresh air that fills my lungs as soon as I open the front door."

Because of its pure prettiness and unfettered femininity, Julie also calls the house her princess palace. With cascading white curtains and a French Empire–style chandelier of antique ormolu and hand-strung crystals, the room resembles a New Orleans debutante decked out in white silk and heirloom jewelry for her presentation. Floor-to-ceiling curtains that match the white walls and equally pale upholstery form an almost minimalist setting that allows moments of texture and detail to shine. In the living room, white mohair pillows and amethyst-colored silk bolsters add fluff and color to two delicate sofas. One antique French and the other a reproduction, the graceful sofas surround a gilded coffee table with Chinese-meets-mid-century-modern lines to create an engaging seating area.

Another Neill chandelier made from salvaged nineteenth-century ormolu banding hangs in the dining room. "When I found the banding, I asked it what it wanted to do," says Julie, who often seems to

ABOVE: *In a corner of the living room, Julie combined a terra-cotta architectural fragment, a Louis XV–style chair with pristine matelassé upholstery and distressed gilt, a marble-topped table, an amethyst geode, and a bright, abstract painting by Amanda Talley.* OPPOSITE: *Furnished mostly in eighteenth- and nineteenth-century European furniture with pale paint and faded gilt, the rooms of Julie's house are airy and uncrowded. Long panels of polished white chintz with valances mounted directly beneath the living room's crown molding contribute to the space's sophisticated simplicity.*

ABOVE: *Julie found a paint-encrusted concrete table base at the now-defunct Carrollton Junque and Antiques Store and had a wood top made to match. The whimsical bronze lamp with over-scale filigree is part of Julie's lighting line.* OPPOSITE: *The designer sanded the gilt finish off two Louis XV chairs down to the gesso. "They were too fancy for the room, so I ruined them a little," she says. Hung between French drawings of chandeliers given to Julie by her friend Vincent Bergeal, a mirror from Antiques on Jackson reflects two chandeliers she designed.*

have conversations with the things she designs. Hanging above a table with legs made from pieces of a cast-iron balcony, also made by Julie, the chandelier helps to bring the twelve-foot-high ceiling down to a more intimate scale.

Unpainted cypress doors open from the dining room into an identical pair of rooms that Julie uses for more relaxed daily living. Shifting the color scheme to cream with touches of amber, Julie warmed the spaces that are illuminated by two more of her chandeliers. With gilded French chairs, a pair of eighteenth-century Italian commodes, and a lit de repos with pillows with antique bullion trim, the rooms are filled with Old World details, as well as occasional pieces of modern art. "My favorite paintings are usually abstract," Julie says. "I like the way they create a rest from antique furniture."

Trained as an artist, Julie made the collaged painting that hangs on the brick chimneypiece in her kitchen. Inspired by an imaginary Greek goddesses dress, its

ABOVE: *Julie's grandmother picked out wedding china for her, purchasing twelve place settings of English Minton china days after she was born. Many years later, the pale pink pattern is still Julie's favorite. "She hadn't even met me and she picked the perfect plates," she marvels.* OPPOSITE: *Rhinestone buttons and dove-gray ribbons from New Orleans' venerable Promenade Fine Fabrics decorate the backs of reproduction Louis XVI chairs in the dining room. Once dark mahogany, the Chippendale china cabinet was a wedding gift from Julie's grandfather. "I thought it would be a sacrilege to paint it," says Julie, who finally lightened it up to match the rest of her luminous decor.*

BELOW: *Julie designed a daybed with extra high sides to create a cozy embrace. "It's such an elegant way to be hugged," she says. Pillows with antique European trim designed by Rebecca Vizard for B. Viz Design contribute to the room's antique style, but an abstract painting by Alabama artist Kent Walsh injects a modern element.* OPPOSITE: *A Neill chandelier with a dozen wax candles adds more Old World romance to the room.*

pattern of pleated folds and Greek key trim are made from confetti-like pieces of paper cut from the pages of Harlequin romance novels. The graceful pavilion-like bed that she designed for her bedroom might have been purloined from a romance novel as well. With eighteenth-century Venetian corner cabinets and pendant lights Julie made by covering 1950s lampshades with a cloud of feathers, the room is enchanting.

Decorating with feathers and fur, crystal and gold, antique iron and painted wood, Julie created a house that is as lighthearted and lovely as her chandeliers. With pale walls, floors, and curtains and large antique mirrors, the rooms seem not only to reflect the natural light but also to create a glow of their own. "I just wanted someplace happy," says Julie, "and happy to me is light, bright, and pretty."

Vintage Thonet chairs surround a country French table in the kitchen where a painting by Julie hangs above an antique iron mantel she purchased on eBay. A pair of plaster-and-iron lanterns inspired by a 1950s design hangs in the hallway behind the kitchen.

Across Time and Place

BETHANY BEACH, DELAWARE

When interior designer Mona Hajj and architect Wayne L. Good joined forces to renovate and redecorate a row house in a 1970s Delaware beachfront development, their starting point was a drab interior with nondescript detail and plenty of what Wayne called "dark Home Depot paneling." Although the residence is located on the edge of the Atlantic Ocean, the architect observed, "If I had been taken there blindfolded, I would have thought I was in the middle of a landlocked commuter suburb." But the clients, who had worked with Mona and Wayne previously, had faith that they could transform it into a charming seaside getaway.

Wayne's first impulse was to lighten up the rooms, both in color and form. Stripping away the Sheetrock and paneling that concealed the beams and studs, he created an open, airy plan on the first floor. Imagining an early twentieth-century beach cottage built by a country carpenter, he applied a modern interpretation of old-fashioned board-and-batten to the walls and opened the ceilings to the floor joists above. Adding a simple blind frieze above the paneling, he created the impression that the ceiling floats above the walls. Once all the wood surfaces were painted white, the space began to shimmer with reflected light.

Inspired by the colors of sand and sea, Mona chose a palette of pale blue, beige, and white for the long living room. Within this serene setting, the Lebanon-born designer combined modern-day furnishings and English antiques with the Mediterranean and Middle Eastern pieces she loves to collect. On one end of the room, an antique Syrian tea table and an English Pembroke table flank a new sofa upholstered in heavy wool chenille. Across the room, a bronze Mediterranean teapot sits on the mantel above a modern fireplace

Architect Wayne Good paneled walls throughout the house with a modern interpretation of board-and-batten siding. The living room's plain mantel with country-carpenter-style knee braces, modern bluestone fire surround, and an antique English wing chair combine the simple with the refined, the antique with the new.

surrounded by shelves holding antique blue-and-white plates from England and China.

In the small family room shared by grandparents, parents, and grandchildren, the interior designer's penchant for combining decorative objects from different countries, periods, and styles finds even fuller expression. "I wanted this room to represent a change in mood from the living room, but still to harmonize with it," says Mona, whose design began with the placement of a boldly striped nineteenth-century Persian kilim on the floor. Next came a brightly patterned Turkish suzani on the wall and an Ottoman-style table upholstered with a faded red Persian carpet. In the midst of these Middle Eastern textiles, a sofa dressed in blue-and-white toile adds an unexpected twist. "As a designer, I put things together," says Mona. "If I love the way they look, then I find a way to make them work."

When Wayne redesigned the floor plan, he relocated the kitchen from the back of the house to its center, tucking the dining area into an alcove across from it. Running an open hallway between the two spaces, he created an easy flow among all the first-floor rooms. To visually unite the areas, Mona decorated the

Wayne and interior designer Mona Hajj worked together to transform a nondescript 1970s beachfront row house into a beautifully detailed home. The living room combines a modern interpretation of Southern vernacular architecture, a contemporary palette, European antiques, and Middle Eastern textiles. A custom rug by Elizabeth Eakins repeats the linear pattern of the board-and-batten walls, unifying the architecture with the interior design.

OPPOSITE: *From the sofa's blue-and-white toile to the bold kilim and antique Turkish suzani, the family room's patterned textiles work together in dynamic energy. Designed by Mona, a versatile table upholstered with an antique rug serves both as an ottoman and a place for stacking books or serving food and drinks on a tray.* BELOW: *An open passageway separates the kitchen from a dining area where a curved alcove embraces the table and those who sit around it. Although the Turkish kilim contrasts with the cool tones of the living room, blue upholstery mirrors the adjoining room's palette. "The colors and tones shift throughout the house, but they all harmonize," Mona says.*

ABOVE: *Wayne relocated the kitchen and united it with the living room by stripping the intervening partition wall down to the studs. Open shelving allows whoever is cooking to converse with those in the living room and look out toward the sea beyond.* OPPOSITE: *Mona used Middle Eastern carpets throughout the house, even in the kitchen, where an antique Persian rug is soft underfoot. With a tongue-and-groove ceiling, vintage-style lighting, and glass-front cabinets, the room recalls the simplicity of a kitchen in an early twentieth-century cottage.*

OPPOSITE: *Mounted above a Chinese box and flanked by iron sconces, an antique Kytak tapestry from Uzbekistan accents the stair landing.* ABOVE: *The soft pink patina of an antique caned bed from France warms up the white walls and ceiling of a guest bedroom. Chosen both for their interesting shapes and small scale, a French table and English chair add character to the room without overcrowding it.*

dining alcove with furniture and textiles that relate to those in the living and family rooms. "Because the floor plan is so open, it was important to make all the rooms work together," she says.

In the dining alcove, the designer combined a nineteenth-century English trestle table with an eighteenth-century French provincial settee and white-painted wood chairs, which though new, have traditional splat backs and turned-wood stretchers. Cushions in several shades of blue and a red-and-taupe kilim echo the palette of the adjoining rooms. Although the 1930s light fixture hanging above the hall comes from Egypt, its opaline shades complement the white glass vintage-style ceiling lights in the kitchen next door.

Upstairs, smaller, more enclosed rooms with lower ceilings offer private sanctuaries for everyone in the house. Although calm in palette and mood, these bedrooms are still rich in texture and pattern. In one, Mona combined a rose-and-grisaille French trumeau mirror with a golden-yellow suzani folded across the foot of a simple painted bed. While pillows with red and gold strips of kilims repeat these glowing colors, an antique English table and Windsor chair introduce natural tones of bamboo and wood to the room.

In another bedroom, the furnishings, artwork, and accessories are mostly Occidental in origin, including a nineteenth-century caned bed and an antique table from France and an English chair. Only a pillow covered with sapphire-colored silk from an antique Indian sari introduces an Eastern touch. Providing an uncomplicated backdrop for the room's antiques, Wayne's subtly modern interpretation of board-and-batten siding balances their formality with vernacular simplicity.

"Because the house is not decorated all in one style, it feels comfortable and collected," Mona explains. "The clients are world travelers and the house expresses this." Despite the worldly nature of its contents, however, the house also possesses the unpretentious charm of a Southern coastal cottage. "If you were to blindfold me again and take me to this house," Wayne says, "I'd be convinced I was in an old-fashioned Delaware beach house when I opened my eyes."

The guest room's simple board-and-batten walls set off the exotic beauty of a Pompeii-inspired trumeau mirror from France and a golden-yellow suzani. Although the pieces were made on two different continents, their graceful patterns have much in common.

Resources

ARCHITECTURE

Norman D. Askins Architect
normanaskins.com
(404) 233-6565

Beau Clowney Design
beauclowney.com
(843) 722-2040

John Deering
Greenline Architecture
greenlinearch.com
(912) 447-5665

Wayne Good
Good Architecture
goodarchitecture.com
(410) 268-7414

Randy Harelson
Richard Gibbs
Richard M. Gibbs Design
(850) 624-8138

Historical Concepts
historicalconcepts.com
(770) 487-8041

McAlpine Tankersley Architecture
mcalpinetankersley.com
(334) 262-8315

Ken Tate Architect
kentatearchitect.com
(985) 845-8181

INTERIOR DESIGN

Joane Askins Interiors
(404) 814-0517

Mona Hajj Interiors
monahajj.com
(410) 234-0091

Amelia T. Handegan, Inc.
athid.com
(843) 722-9373

Carter Kay Interiors
carterkayinteriors.com
(404) 261-8119

Jacquelynne P. Lanham Designs
jackyelanham.com
(404) 364-0472

Regina Lynch
Ecru Antiques & Interiors
ecruantiques.com
(504) 304-9475

Lynn Morgan
lynnmorgandesign.com
(203) 866-1940

Tracery Interiors
traceryinteriors.com
(850) 231-6755

Melanie Turner
melanieturnerinteriors.com
(404) 250-0134

Suzanne Rester Watson
inside-inc.com
(850) 685-5504

GARDENS

Richard Anderson
richardandersonla.com
(404) 892-1788

Ryan Gainey
ryangainey.com
(404) 377-1494

Goodness Grows
Goodnessgrows.com
(706) 743-5055

Roses Unlimited
Rosesunlimitedownroot.com
(864) 682-7673

Wertimer & Associates
wertimer.com
(843) 577-3360

ART

Justin Gaffrey
justingaffrey.com
(850) 267-2022

Maggie Grier
maggiegrier.com
(205) 401-1719

Timothy McDowell
tjmcdowell@mac.com
(860) 572-4489

Tony Mose
esomart.com
(225) 202-6406

Amanda Stone Talley
amandatalley.com
(504) 595-3136

Ulises Toache
toache.com
(678) 361-0663

Kent Walsh
kentwalshartist.com
(251) 929-2576

DECORATIVE PAINTING

Anne Bielowicz
(404) 210-7874

Kristen Bunting Decorative Arts
kristenbunting@comcast.net
(843) 830-3373

Bob Christian Decorative Art
bobchristiandecorativeart.com
(912) 234-1960

Howell Jones
(404) 874-4048

ANTIQUES

A. Tyner Antiques
Swedishantiques.biz
(404) 367-4484

Agora
Agoragalleries.com
(504) 525-2240

Alex Raskin Antiques
alexraskinantiques.com
(912) 232-8205

Antiques and Beyond
antiquesandbeyond.com
(404) 872-4342

Antiques on Jackson
(504) 524-8201

Au Vieux Paris Antiques
auvieuxparisantiques.com
(337) 332-2852

Bush Antiques
bushantiques.com
(504) 581-3518

Foxglove Antiques and Galleries
foxgloveantiques.com
(888) 800-4369

Henhouse Antiques
shophenhouseantiques.com
(205) 918-0505

Karla Katz Antiques
karlakatzandco.1stdibs.com
(504) 897-0061

Neal Auction Company
nealauction.com
(800) 467-5329

Nicole Maleine French Antiques
nicolemaleinefrenchantiques.com
(334) 834-8530

A perfume bottle that belonged to her grandmother, a fluted silver vase from her great-grandmother, and a box of stationery imported by her husband are among the objects that add charm to interior designer Lynn Morgan's writing table.

Scott Antique Market
Scottantiquemarket.com
(404) 361-2000

Uptowner Antiques
uptownerantiques.com
(504) 891-7700

FURNITURE AND ACCESSORIES

A&P Iron Designs
apirondesigns.vacau.com
(770) 941-0082

Abigails
Abigails.net
(800) 678-8485

Ross Askins Specialty Carpentry
(205) 807-7677

Julian Chichester
julianchichester.com
(336) 886 2454

Ecru Antiques & Interiors
(see Interior Design)

Eloquence
eloquenceinc.com
(310) 453-5503

The Ryan Gainey Collection
Jeremie
jeremiecorp.com
(888) 537-3643

Mainly Baskets
mainlybaskets.com
(404) 634-7664

McAlpine Home Collection
leeindustries.com
(800) 892-7150

MacRae Designs
macraedesigns.com
(800) 446-5526

Mrs. Howard
mrshoward.com
(404) 816-3830

Peacock Pavers
peacockpavers.com
(800) 264-2072

Charles P. Rogers
charlesprogers.com
(800) 582-6229

Carolina Rustica
carolinarustica.com
(800) 205-7819

South of Market
southofmarket.biz
(404) 995-9399

M A Williams Furniture Makers
(404) 895-9980

Wisteria
wisteria.com
(800) 320-9757

LIGHTING

Circa Lighting
circalighting.com
(877) 762-2323

Edgar Reeves Lighting and Antiques
edgar-reeves.com
(404) 237-1137

Eloise Pickard
eloipck9@aol.com
(770) 324-2557

Gates Moore Lighting
gatesmoorelighting.com
(203) 847-3231

Julie Neill Designs
julieneill.com
(504) 899-4201

TEXTILES

B. Berger
bberger.com
(330) 425-3838

B Viz Design
bviz.com
(318) 766-4950

Groves Bros. Fabrics
grovesbros.com
(817) 921-4450

Keivan Woven Arts
keivanwovenarts.com
(404) 266-3336

Leontine Linens
leontinelinens.com
(800) 876-4799

Pandora de Balthazar
pandoradebalthazar.com
(850) 432-4777

Romo
romo.com
(800) 338-2783

Shabby Slips
Shabbyslipsrosemarybeach.com
(850) 231-4164

Zimmer-Rohde
zimmer-rohde.com
(203) 327-1400

COMMUNITIES

The Ford Plantation
fordplantation.com
(912) 756-5666

Rosemary Beach
rosemarybeach.com
(800) 736-0877